TABLE OF C

M000289447

For my husband, Charlie, and our children,
Beth, Charles and Fitz, with my love.

With grateful appreciation to: ALL those who so willingly shared their recipes – • – MARGARET ALMOND for her invaluable assistance, sustained enthusiasm and untiring effort – • – BETH for her confidence, encouragement and copy editing – • – CHARLES for the format suggestions and his business acumen – • – FITZ for the divider page drawings and his artistic advice – • – CHARLIE for his tangible support and willingness to "try anything once".

Special thanks: *Consultants:* Bill DeGain and Cindy Bibb of Insty Prints, Richmond, Virginia. *1992 New Cover Design:* The Wimmer Companies, Memphis, TN 38181. *Photograph:* Trevor Wrayton, Richmond, Virginia.

INTRODUCTION

IT'S 5 O'CLOCK – the working day is done – the family gathers – dinner time approaches – How many times have you asked yourself as you wander into the kitchen, *"What in the world are we going to have for dinner?"* If this questions sounds all too familiar and the answer a bit disappointing, then this book is for you.

With the active lifestyles of today, cooks are finding they have less and less time to spend in the kitchen. In order to make the most of the time you have, there is no substitute for pre-planning and organization. A quick pantry check (see Basic Pantry Stock) plus the underlined items in the recipes complete your shopping list for that meal. By having all the ingredients on hand and doing some preparation ahead, you can relax and enjoy a less hectic pre-dinner hour.

It is our hope that with the help of this book, when 5 o'clock comes around you will never again ask yourself, *"What in the world are we going to have for dinner?"* and be disappointed.

Beth/Sarah

The recipes in this book are a collection; very few are my originals. Family and friends have been most willing to share their favorites. Recipes have been collected through the years from magazines, newspapers and a wide variety of cookbooks, especially Junior League cookbooks which I have collected from near and far. I encourage you to share recipes and ideas. Many recipes do not include the number of servings; increase or decrease according to the needs of your family. All directions are given for the conventional oven; adaptation to your microwave is encouraged. Don't hesitate to try something new or to substitue an ingredient with one you find more pleasing. To quote one of my favorite chefs: *"Cooking is not like chemistry class!"* So, have fun and enjoy . . .

Sarah

🐾 INDICATES EARLY STEPS ARE REQUIRED.

5

HELPFUL HINTS
and
TIME SAVING TIPS

1. Use the Basic Pantry Stock check list and the underlined items in these recipes to make a complete shopping list.

2. Cook several pounds of ground beef at once and freeze in one pound packages. It is good to use in spaghetti sauces and casseroles.

3. Freeze left-over vegetables to use in soups and stews. Rice freezes especially well. Be sure to label, date and place in one certain spot in the freezer for easy accessability.

4. Grate whole blocks of cheese and freeze in ½ C and 1 C packages. Defrost on a paper towel.

5. Meaure ½ tsp and 1 tsp of salt in your palm so you don't have to get out measuring spoons each time.

6. Add instant mashed potatoes to soups to thicken.

7. Whole nutmeg freshly grated is more flavorful.

8. Try to make large cakes or batches of cookies toward the end of the week to carry over into the weekend.

9. Save crusts of bread for bread crumbs. Spread crusts on baking sheet and bake at 350 degrees for 10 - 15 minutes or until dry enough to crumble.

10. Evaporated milk may be substituted for half and half or light cream in most recipes.

11. When possible, allow beef to come to room temperature before cooking.

12. Prepare double portions and freeze the extra for a ready meal another time. Also, keep single serving left-overs wrapped and labeled in the freezer for an unexpected hot lunch or a child's supper on Mom's night out.

13. Grate orange and lemon rinds before cutting the fruit. A zester is a marvelous gadget. Zest or grate over the dish being prepared so the oils sprayed out will not be lost but will further enhance the flavor.

14. When adding flour to liquids, place flour in jar with water and shake briskly until lumps dissolve.

6

15. Sweet milk can be soured by adding 1 Tbsp vinegar, 1 Tbsp cream of tartar or 1 Tbsp lemon juice to 1 cup milk. Allow to stand 3 - 5 minutes, stir, then use as buttermilk in recipes.

16. For ice molds with flowers or fruits: place flowers or fruit in bottom of mold with little bit of water. Freeze, then add water to fill mold. This will hold flowers or fruit in the bottom, i.e. the top when inverted in a punch bowl.

17. For recipes that call for cooked julienne strips or sliced carrots, cook carrots whole, then they are much easier to cut or slice.

18. For finely chopped nuts or crackers, drop into blender at high speed. May need to repeat.

19. Use a wire pastry blender to chop hard cooked eggs.

20. Get air out of zip-lock bags with a straw.

21. A good *"job"* for children is to set and clear the table.

22. When marinating for long periods, place meat and marinade into a tightly closed plastic bag. No turning needed.

23. Split cake layers with thread. Wrap around the middle of the outside edge and pull through.

24. Lemon juice or fruit-fresh sprinkled over fruit will prevent it from browning after being cut. Ex. apples, avocados, and peaches.

25. To keep parsley *"like-fresh"*: chop fresh parsley, mix with small amount of water and freeze in ice cube tray. Store cubes in plastic bag in freezer. Plop one or two cubes in soups and sauces or thaw on a paper towel. Ice will melt, leaving like-fresh parsley.

26. Plant herbs and vegetables at home. It makes a lovely addition to your flower beds and picking them for the table is not only fun but tasty and economical. Parsley, chives, and leaf lettuce are especially carefree; basil, dill and cocktail tomatoes (although need more sun) mix well with flowers.

27. Use parsley in salads as well as for garnish. It is very rich in iron.

28. Run hot water over a lemon before squeezing to soften rind.

29. Keep aluminum pie pans for freezing casseroles.

30. To save time unloading the dishwasher, put all forks, knives, etc. in separate sections. Saves sorting out when putting away.

31. Spay oil in pot in which pasta is to be cooked before adding water. Helps prevent sticking. Spray oil on water surface of pasta pot or add pat of butter before adding pasta. Prevents clumping and sticking together.

32. A good place to let dough rise is in the oven with door cracked open - free from drafts.

33. To *"dust"* with powdered sugar or cocoa, spoon powder into a small strainer and tap gently over surface.

34. To refresh wilted parsley: fill bowl with warm water, submerge parsley in water for 10 - 15 seconds. Make fresh cut on stems and immediately put in glass of water. Gently shake water from parsley leaves then cover in plastic bag securing around the base of glass with a rubber band. Refrigerate.

35. Stand stuffed peppers or tomatoes for baking in greased muffin tins. Holds them upright.

36. For *"old"* recipes it's good to know that 1 lb. flour = 4 C and 1 lb. granulated sugar = 2 C.

37. Encourage other family members to do outdoor cooking on the grill. It's a big help and fun for them.

38. In buying fresh fruits and vegetables, look for firmness and good color. Avoid ones that are limp, discolored or spotted. Honeydew melons are ripe when rind has a creamy yellowish appearance.

39. Coat meat in flour mixture by shaking one or two pieces at a time in a plastic bag or lunch-size brown paper bag.

40. Use celery, water chestnuts, almonds or other nuts to add crunchiness for a contrast in textures.

41. Keep a one teaspoon measuring spoon in the box of baking soda and baking powder.

42. Cup cake papers make good individual congealed salad molds. Set papers in muffin tins to fill. Peel the paper off to serve.

43. Unwrap sticks of butter and allow to soften in the mixing bowl. This saves having to get soft butter off of paper.

44. Keep infrequently used items in the freezer to retain freshness; such as corn meals, flours, coffees, nuts and coconut for baking.

BASIC PANTRY STOCK

BAKING ITEMS

baking powder
baking soda
cooking oil
corn meal
  white
  yellow
  self-rising
flour
  plain
  self-rising
  whole wheat
pepper
  black
  fresh-ground
  white
salt
shortening
sugar
  granulated
  brown
  confectioners
yeast

DAIRY PRODUCTS

butter
cheese
  sharp
  parmesan
eggs
margarine
milk
  table and cooking
    (whole, 2% or
    skim)
  evaporated
  dry mix
  buttermilk
sour cream

HERBS and SPICES

allspice
basil
caraway seed
cayenne pepper
celery salt
celery seed
chives
cinnamon
  ground
  stick
cloves
  ground
  whole
dill
  leaf
  seed
extracts
  lemon
  orange
  vanilla
garlic salt
ginger - ground
lemon pepper
mustard - dry
nutmeg - ground
onion flakes
onion juice
onion salt
oregano
paprika
parsley flakes
rosemary
sesame seeds
tarragon
thyme

FREQUENTLY USED ITEMS

Accent
biscuit mix
bouillon
  instant or cubed
  beef
  chicken
catsup
celery
corn starch
fresh fruit in season
graham cracker
 crumbs
green salad fixings
lettuce
lemons
mayonnaise
mustard
  Dijon
  prepared - yellow
no-stick cooking
 spray
onion
  green scallions
  yellow
rice
salad dressings
salad oil
soy sauce
vinegar
  cider
  red wine
  tarragon
  white wine
Worcestershire
 sauce

NOTES

WINTER

WINTER

MAIN DISHES

Chicken Divan • Marinated Pork Tenderloin • Baked Lasagna • Carefree Pot Roast • Ham Steak with Raisin Sauce • Chicken with Sour Cream • Shrimp Stir Fry • Marinated Flank Steak • Rump Roast • Hamburger Quiche • Frosted Meat Loaf • Brunswick Stew • Sausage and Wild Rice • Shrimp Creole • Beef Burgundy • Sweet and Sour Beef Chunks • Shrimp • Marinated Pork Roast • Herbed Chicken • Chicken Pot Pie

VEGETABLES

Carrots with Mustard Sauce • Scalloped Potatoes • Green Peas • Sautéed Green Beans • Sweet Potatoes • Broccoli • Rice with Celery • Snow Peas • Frosted Cauliflower • French-Cut Green Beans • Broccoli with Hollandaise • Carrots • Broccoli with Cheese Whiz • Cheese Rice • Rice • Broiled Tomatoes • Speedy Spinach • Broccoli Casserole • Potato Bake

SALADS

Sliced Pineapple • Chunky Applesauce • Tossed Salad with Italian Dressing • Grapefruit and Avocado • Sliced Peaches • Slaw • Jellied Applesauce • Fresh Green • Raw Vegetable • Tossed • Sliced Lettuce • Hot Peaches • Blueberry

BREADS

Popovers • Mock Monkey • Toasted Garlic • Angel Biscuits • Gingerbread Muffins • Buttermilk Muffins • Toasted Pita • Refrigerator Biscuits • Southern Spoon Bread • Drop Biscuits • Sausage Pinwheels • Six Week Muffins • Quick Little Loaf • Crescent Rolls • Beer Bread • Corn Muffins • Biscuits

DESSERTS

Reese's Pieces Cookies • Potato Chip Cookies • Pistachio Mousse • Peppermint Whip Pie • Fruit Fluff • Cherry Pudding • Prune Cake • Purple Plum Cake • Baked Apples • "Mock" Cheese Cake • Toffee Bars • Raw Apple Cake • Apple Spice Bars • Lemon Cookies • Date-Nut Bars • Chocolate Chess Pie • Lemon Pie • Cherry Crunch • Scotch Shortbread • Chocolate Chip Cake

CHICKEN DIVAN

1 pkg (10 oz) frozen broccoli
4 whole chicken breasts
1 can cream of chicken soup
½ C mayonnaise
½ lemon - juiced
½ tsp curry powder
½ C soft bread crumbs
4 Tbsp butter melted
½ C grated sharp cheese

Cook chicken in salted water until tender. Remove. Put on paper towels to drain. Drop broccoli in same water and cook just until heated. Drain. In a sprayed casserole dish make single layer of broccoli. Cut each chicken breast into several pieces and arrange on top of broccoli. Make sauce of soup, mayonnaise, lemon juice and curry. Pour over chicken. Mix butter and bread crumbs. (See helpful Hint # 9.) Spread cheese over bread crumbs. Bake in 350 degree oven for about 20 minutes or until thoroughly heated and cheese melts. Serves 4 - 6.

1966 - Yvonne Dipple
Bettendorf, Iowa

SLICED PINEAPPLE SALAD

1 large can sliced pineapple
lettuce
grated cheese

Arrange pineapple slice on bed of lettuce. Garnish with mayonnaise and grated cheese.

14

CARROTS with MUSTARD SAUCE

3 C carrots
1 Tbsp prepared mustard
3 Tbsp brown sugar
2 Tbsp butter or margarine - melted

Clean enough carrots to make 3 cups. (See helpful hint # 17.) Boil in lightly salted water, just until tender. Drain and slice. Combine melted butter with sugar and mustard. Pour over carrots and lightly toss. Serves 4 - 6.

Mrs. Wyatt French

POPOVERS

1 C flour
1 C milk
¼ tsp salt
2 eggs
1 Tbsp cooking oil

Add eggs, milk and oil to blender. Blend at high speed for several seconds. Turn blender to medium high speed and add flour and salt. Blend only until smooth being careful to scrape flour from sides. Fill hot greased muffin tins ½ full. Bake in preheated 450 degree oven for 10 minutes. Reduce heat to 350 degrees for 20 minutes. Keep oven door closed throughout. Makes 12.

REESE'S PIECES COOKIES

1 roll peanut-butter slice and bake cookie dough
1 pkg mini-Reese's peanut-butter cups
paper liners for mini-muffin tins

Slice cookie dough very thin. Place a candy in the center and fold up sides. Place this in a paper liner and then in mini-muffin tins. Cookies resemble little tarts. Bake at 400 degrees for 10 - 12 minutes or until cookie is firm and brown around the edges.

Mother, Elizabeth F. Easley
Danville, Virginia

> ❧ MARINATED PORK TENDERLOIN
>
> SCALLOPED POTATOES   GREEN PEAS
>
> CHUNKY APPLESAUCE
>
> MOCK MONKEY BREAD
>
> ❧ POTATO CHIP COOKIES

MARINATED PORK TENDERLOIN

2 <u>whole pork tenderloins</u>
2 slices <u>bacon</u>

MARINADE:

½ C soy sauce
1 Tbsp vinegar
¼ tsp cayenne

½ tsp sugar
1 Tbsp grated onion
1 <u>garlic clove minced</u>

Wrap tenderloins in bacon and secure with wooden tooth picks. Mix marinade ingredients and pour over tenderloins. Marinate several hours turning occasionally. (See helpful hint # 22.) Marinating all day is not too long. Remove meat from marinade. Place in greased shallow baking dish. Bake uncovered at 350 degrees for 1½ hours. Baste occasionally with marinade. Turn once during cooking time. Serves 6.

Heat marinade and serve as sauce with meat.

SCALLOPED POTATOES

1 can <u>cream of celery soup</u>
⅔ C <u>evaporated milk</u>
4 C <u>white potatoes</u> - thinly sliced
1 onion - thinly sliced or dried onion flakes
butter or margarine
salt and pepper

Mix condensed soup with milk. In a sprayed casserole dish make several layers in the following order: soup mixture, potato slices, sprinkle with onion or onion flakes, dot with butter, salt and pepper. Bake 1 hour and 20 - 30 minutes at 350 degrees. Leftovers may be frozen. Serves 4 - 6.

PEAS - Use your favorite canned or frozen <u>peas</u> and cook as directed. (I prefer LeSueur canned peas.)

CHUNKY APPLESAUCE

6 - 8 <u>golden delicious apples</u>
salt
sugar
cinnamon

Peel and quarter apples. In heavy saucepan put enough water in bottom to cover. Add apples and simmer until tender. Watch closely and stir occasionally. When cooked, add sugar to taste and a dash of salt. Add a few shakes of ground cinnamon if desired. Serve warm or cold. Refrigerate any leftovers. Keeps well.

MOCK MONKEY BREAD

1 pkg <u>refrigerator biscuits</u>
½ stick butter - melted

Cut biscuits in quarters and roll in melted butter. (Use more if needed.) Put biscuit pieces in a small sprayed loaf pan overlapping edges. Bake at 350 degrees for 15 minutes or until golden brown. Serve on platter. Pull off pieces.

POTATO CHIP COOKIES

1 lb. butter - softened
1½ C sugar
3½ C flour
2 tsp vanilla
1 C <u>pecan pieces</u>
1½ C <u>crushed potato chips</u>

Cream butter and sugar. Add remaining ingredients with chips being last. Mix well. Drop by teaspoonfuls on greased cookie sheet. Bake at 350 degrees for 15 - 18 minutes. Keeps well in cookie tin with tight fitting top.

"These are really good."
Margie Ayres

17

BAKED LASAGNA

TOSSED GREEN SALAD

ITALIAN DRESSING

TOASTED GARLIC BREAD

PISTACHIO MOUSSE

LASAGNA

lasagna noodles
1 large jar spaghetti sauce with mushrooms
1 tsp Italian seasoning mix
1 tsp oregano
1 tsp salt
1 small onion - chopped or 1 Tbsp dried onion flakes
1 lb cooked ground beef
1 carton (16 oz) cottage cheese
1 egg
sliced mozarella cheese
grated parmesan cheese

Cook noodles according to package directions. Rinse under cold water. Mix spaghetti sauce, ground beef, (See helpful hint # 2.) onion, and seasonings. Beat egg and mix with cottage cheese. In a large baking dish layer as follows: thin layer sauce mixture, single layer of cooked noodles, sauce mixture, sliced mozarella cheese, cooked noodles, cottage cheese mixture, cooked noodles, sauce mixture, sliced mozarella cheese, grated parmesan cheese. Bake at 350 degrees until thoroughly hot and cheese begins to brown. This freezes well - actually better the second time. Additional parmesan cheese may be added at the table. Serves 8.

TOSSED GREEN SALAD with ITALIAN DRESSING

For the salad, use a mixture of lettuce and fresh vegetables. Our favorite dressing is Good Seasons Italian mix. Follow package directions, then add a generous dash of sugar.

Jane Wootton

GARLIC BREAD

whole loaf of Italian bread
or
split hamburger or hot dog rolls (good way to finish a partially used package)

Slice loaf or rolls lengthwise. Spread with softened butter. Sprinkle with garlic salt. Broil in oven until toasted. Slice into individual size pieces to serve.

PISTACHIO MOUSSE

1 pkg instant pudding mix - pistachio
1½ C milk
1 C frozen whipped topping - thawed

Mix pudding mix and milk in a jar or container with tight fitting lid. Shake vigorously until smooth - about half a minute. Fold in the whipped topping. Fill serving dishes and refrigerate until serving time. For variety, any of the following might be added: 1 small can drained crushed pineapple, chopped maraschino cherries, chopped nuts, or mini-marshmallows. Serves 4.

"Have this meal on the day you'll be late.
Use the oven timer for the roast."

POT ROAST

3 - 4 lb boneless pot roast
¼ **tsp pepper**
1 Tbsp instant beef bouillon
6 - 8 small potatoes - peeled and left whole
6 - 8 carrots - peeled and left whole
1 small onion - sliced
1 can (10 oz) cream of onion soup
1 can (10 oz) cream of celery soup
1 can (10 oz) cream of tomato soup
heavy duty aluminum foil

Line baking dish with large piece of aluminum foil. Place roast in center of foil. Rub pepper and bouillon on top of roast. Place onion on top of roast and potatoes and carrots around edge. Pour undiluted soups over roast. Tightly seal roast in foil. Bake at 300 degrees for 4½ hours. Set timer on oven. Serves 6 - 8.

FRESH GREEN BEANS - washed and trimmed

Leave whole. Melt butter in sauce pan. Add green beans. Sauté until thoroughly heated and barely lost bright green color, about 5 minutes. Transfer to serving dish. Salt to taste.

ANGEL BISCUITS

*"This can be made ahead and frozen in one-meal packages.
It makes a lot – will do for many meals. Dough also keeps
well in refrigerator in tight container."*

5 C unsifted flour
¼ C sugar
3 tsp baking powder
1 tsp baking soda
2 tsp salt
1 C solid shortening
1 pkg dry yeast
2 Tbsp warm water
2 C buttermilk

Sift dry ingredients together. Cut in shortening with a pastry
blender. Dissolve yeast in warm water then add to buttermilk.
Combine liquid mixture with dry ingredients. Use dough hooks to
mix. Turn dough onto floured surface and roll to about ½ inch
thick. Cut with a biscuit cutter. Place on a lightly greased flat pan.
Bake at 475 degrees for 10 minutes or until brown. Makes about
4 dozen.

1982 - Frances Wimbush Jones

PEPPERMINT WHIP PIE

"Great way to use Christmas candy canes."

14 plain chocolate wafers
½ pt. whipping cream
1¼ C mini marshmallows
½ C crushed peppermint candy

Crush wafers and spread evenly in bottom of a 9 x 11 inch
pan. Whip cream. Add in marshmallows and crushed candy.
(Children love to help with this. Wrap candy in non-terry cloth
towel and let them hammer!) Spoon mixture onto chocolate
wafer crumbs. May sprinkle a few additional crumbs on top for
decoration. Refrigerate at least an hour before serving. Serves 6.

Louise Williams

HAM STEAKS with RAISIN SAUCE

ham steaks - amount needed

Trim excess fat from edges of steaks. Broil about 5 minutes per side.

SAUCE:
½ C raisins
1 stick butter or margarine
½ C brown sugar

Soak raisins in warm water until soft - about 15 minutes. Melt butter. Add brown sugar and heat until bubbling. Add drained raisins. Keep warm until serving time. A few tablespoons of pan drippings adds to flavor of sauce. Serve in a sauce bowl with ham.

BAKED SWEET POTATOES

sweet potatoes - one whole potato for each person

Wash potatoes and pat dry. Rub with bacon drippings or margarine. Prick skin with a fork. Bake 1 hour at 350 degrees. Serve with lots of butter.

BROCCOLI

fresh broccoli - 1 bunch usually serves 2
½ stick butter or margarine - melted

Place broccoli on steaming rack in a pot over boiling water. Cover and allow to steam about 5 minutes. Broccoli should be bright green and "crisp" tender. Transfer to serving bowl. Pour melted butter over broccoli and toss lightly. Salt to taste.

GINGERBREAD MUFFINS

1 C shortening
1 C sugar
1 C dark molasses
4 eggs
2 tsp soda
1 C buttermilk
4 C flour
1 Tbsp plus 1 tsp ground ginger
1 tsp allspice
½ tsp nutmeg

Cream shortening; gradually add sugar beating until light and fluffy. Stir in molasses. Add eggs, one at a time, beating well after each addition. Dissolve soda in buttermilk. Combine flour and spices; add to the creamed mixture alternately with buttermilk, beating well after each addition. Cover and store in refrigerator until ready to bake. (Batter will keep in refrigerator for 6 weeks.) Spoon batter into greased muffin pans. Bake at 350 degrees for 20 minutes. Yield: 4 dozen.

Jane Wootton

FRUIT FLUFF

1 pkg instant lemon pudding mix
1 large can pineapple chunks with juice
1 large can fruit cocktail with juice
1 can mandarin oranges - drained
1 pkg frozen whole strawberries
bananas

Add pudding mix to pineapple and fruit cocktail juices. Stir to mix. Add fruits, the drained mandarin oranges and strawberries. (Fresh strawberries may be used if desired.) Refrigerate before serving. (Refrigerate cans of fruit ahead to reduce chilling time.) Sliced bananas may be added at serving time.

1980 - Kathleen Kirk (Mrs. Charles)
Winston-Salem, North Carolina

CHICKEN with SOUR CREAM

RICE with CELERY

GREEN BEANS with TARRAGON

BUTTERMILK MUFFINS

CHERRY PUDDING

CHICKEN with SOUR CREAM

6 chicken breast halves
fine cracker crumbs (optional)

SAUCE:

2 cups sour cream
2 tsp paprika
2 tsp celery salt
2 Tbsp lemon juice
½ tsp garlic salt
2 Tbsp Worcestershire sauce

Remove skin from chicken pieces. Wash and pat dry. Mix all sauce ingredients together. May be made up to one day ahead and refrigerated. Dip chicken pieces in sour cream mixture, then place in a foil-lined shallow baking dish. Sprinkle with cracker crumbs if desired. Bake at 350 degrees for 1 hour. Serves 4 - 6.

RICE with CELERY

rice
½ C celery - chopped

Prepare your favorite rice in the amount needed. Add celery to boiling water along with rice. Celery adds flavor and a "crunchy" to rice.

GREEN BEANS with TARRAGON

fresh green beans
¼ **tsp dried tarragon flakes**

Wash and trim fresh green beans. Leave whole. Place steaming rack over boiling water. Steam green beans for about 10 minutes - until they are crisp-tender. Remove to serving dish. Toss lightly with butter or margarine, tarragon and salt to taste.

BUTTERMILK MUFFINS

1 C self-rising flour
¼ tsp soda
1 egg - beaten
1 C buttermilk

Combine buttermilk (See helpful hint # 15.) and soda. Add flour, stirrring until smooth. Beat in egg. Pour into greased muffin tins. Bake at 425 degrees for 30 - 40 minutes. Makes 6.

CHERRY PUDDING

1 can (16 oz) **red pitted cherries**
1½ C sugar - divided
½ C milk
1 tsp baking powder
¼ tsp salt
1 C flour
2 Tbsp butter or margarine

Mix cherries and juice with 1 cup sugar. Stir until sugar is dissolved. Mix ½ cup sugar, baking powder, salt and flour with milk. Stir until smooth. Melt butter in an 8 inch pyrex dish. Spread batter evenly in dish. Pour cherry mixture over batter. Bake for 45 - 50 minutes at 350 degrees. Do not over bake. Serves 4 - 6.

SHRIMP STIR-FRY
SNOW PEAS
TOASTED PITA BREAD
❧ PRUNE CAKE

SHRIMP STIR-FRY

1 lb. small cooked shrimp - may be frozen
2 Tbsp oil - for wok
1 C chopped green onion - more for garnish
½ - ¾ C sliced fresh mushrooms
1 can water chestnuts - sliced and drained
½ tsp sugar
¼ C soy sauce
2 C cooked rice - cold

In large frying pan or wok, heat oil. Sauté onions and fresh mushrooms until soft. Add water chestnuts and cook one minute. Stir in rice and mix well. Add sugar, soy sauce and shrimp. Continue stirring until thoroughly heated and golden brown. Transfer to serving platter and garnish with chopped green onions. Serves 4 - 6.

SNOW PEAS - Wash and trim fresh snow pea pods. Melt butter in pan large enough to allow stirring. Sauté pea pods in butter until thoroughly heated but still crisp. Transfer to serving dish and salt to taste. Servings of snow peas need not be large. It is more of an accompaniment to the stir-fry.

TOASTED PITA BREAD

pita bread
onion salt

Cut pita rounds apart with scissors. Spread rounds with soft butter and sprinkle with onion salt. Toast under broiler. Cut into wedges to serve. Use white or whole wheat pita bread.

PRUNE CAKE

"This is a great sheet cake. I take it to picnics and the beach in an aluminum throwaway pan. There never is any left to bring home."

1½ C sugar
1 C oil
3 eggs
2 C flour
1 tsp soda
1 tsp cinnamon
1 tsp nutmeg
1 tsp allspice
1 tsp salt
1 C buttermilk
1 tsp vanilla
1 jar <u>cooked prunes</u> - pitted, drained and chopped
1 C <u>chopped nuts</u> (pecans or walnuts)

Beat sugar and oil together. Add eggs one at a time and beat well. Add dry ingredients and liquids alternately, then prunes and nuts. Pour into a greased and floured large sheet cake pan. Bake at 300 degrees for 1 hour and ten minutes.

While cake is baking make icing and keep warm.

ICING:

1 C sugar
1 stick butter or margarine
½ tsp soda
½ tsp vanilla
1 Tbsp <u>Karo syrup</u>
¼ C buttermilk

Mix all ingredients together in heavy sauce pan and boil hard stirring constantly for 2 - 3 minutes until thickened. Keep warm and pour over cake as soon as it is removed from the oven.

This cake is good served warm or cold.

1969 - Etta Mae Neal
Danville, Virginia

&. MARINATED FLANK STEAK
FROSTED CAULIFLOWER
FRENCH - CUT GREEN BEANS
GRAPEFRUIT and AVOCADO SALAD
REFRIGERATOR BISCUIT LOAF
&. PURPLE PLUM CAKE

MARINATED FLANK STEAK

1½ - 2 lbs flank steak

MARINADE:

¾ C vegetable oil
¼ C soy sauce
⅛ tsp garlic salt
¼ tsp ginger

½ C honey
2 Tbsp red wine vinegar
2 Tbsp grated onion

Place steak in shallow pan. Combine marinade ingredients and pour over steak. Cover and refrigerate at least 4 hours. May be done night before. (See helpful hint # 22.) Remove meat from marinade and broil 5 minutes per side. Cut in thin cross-grain strips to serve. Marinade may be heated and served as sauce.

FROSTED CAULIFLOWER

1 medium head cauliflower
salt
½ C mayonnaise

2 tsp prepared mustard
¾ C grated sharp cheese

Wash and trim leaves from the whole head of cauliflower. Par boil in lightly salted water for 12 - 15 minutes. Remove and drain. Place cauliflower in baking dish lined with foil which will allow head to stand upright. Sprinkle with salt. Mix mayonnaise and mustard and spread over cauliflower. Top with grated cheese. Place in 375 degree oven for about 10 minutes or until cheese melts. Cut in wedges to serve. Serves 6.

FRENCH-CUT GREEN BEANS - Heat canned or frozen <u>French cut beans</u> in small amount of water. Add 1 Tbsp butter and ½ cup <u>slivered almonds</u>. Simmer 5 - 7 minutes. Salt to taste.

GRAPEFRUIT and AVOCADO SALAD

2 <u>avocado</u> - should be soft to touch
2 <u>grapefruit</u>
<u>French dressing</u>

Peel grapefruit and cut out sections. Peel and slice avocado. Toss lightly with bottled French dressing. Serve on bed of lettuce or in fruit bowls. Serves 4 - 6.

REFRIGERATOR BISCUIT LOAF

1 can <u>refrigerator biscuits</u>
½ stick butter - melted
2 Tbsp sesame seeds

Cut biscuits in half and layer with rounded ends overlapping in small baking dish or loaf pan. Drizzle melted butter over biscuits and sprinkle with sesame seeds. Bake according to package directions.

PURPLE PLUM CAKE

"This cake keeps well and is a favorite for dessert and snacks."

2 C sugar
3 eggs
2 C self-rising flour
1 tsp cinnamon
1 tsp nutmeg
1 tsp allspice

1 C vegetable oil
1 jar <u>Gerber Junior plums with tapioca</u>
1 C chopped <u>nuts</u> (optional)
powdered sugar

Combine all ingredients and mix at medium speed. Do not over beat. Pour batter into greased and floured bundt pan. Bake at 350 degrees for 45 - 50 minutes. Cool cake on a rack. Invert on cake plate and sprinkle top with powdered sugar. (See helpful hint # 33.)

Sara S. Erickson

29

RUMP ROAST

3 lb rump roast
¾ C cooking sherry

Sear roast on all sides in a small amount of cooking oil. When browned add cooking sherry to roasting pan. Cover tightly and roast at 350 degrees for about 2½ hours. (Set oven timer to come on if necessary.) Check once or twice during cooking time to see if more liquid is needed. When done, allow roast to stand about 10 minutes before slicing.

GRAVY: Stir 2 Tbsp flour into 2 Tbsp melted butter until smooth. Stir in 1½ C   liquids - include pan drippings, a tablespoon of cooking sherry, a tablespoon of instant beef bouillon, then water to make 1½ C. Cook, stirring constantly, until thickened. Serves 4.

Eva Easley
Bluefield, West Virginia

BROCCOLI with HOLLANDAISE - Wash and trim fresh broccoli. Steam over boiling water 5 - 6 minutes.

HOLLANDAISE SAUCE:

3 Tbsp butter	**½ tsp salt**
2 Tbsp flour	**2 eggs - well beaten**
1 C boiling water	**dash cayenne pepper**
1½ Tbsp lemon juice	

Melt butter in top of double boiler. Add flour and stir until smooth. Add boiling water. Continue stirring until thickened. Add remaining ingredients and continue to cook, stirring continuously, until it is of sauce consistency. Pour immediately over steamed broccoli.

Susie Easley Early by Eva Easley
Bluefield, West Virginia

SOUTHERN SPOON BREAD

"This doesn't take as long as it sounds and is well worth the effort."

2 C milk	**2 Tbsp butter or margarine**
1 C white corn meal	**3 eggs - separated**
1 Tbsp salt	**2 tsp baking powder**

Scald milk in a heavy sauce pan over medium high heat. Gradually stir in corn meal. Cook until smooth and thickened. Remove from heat. Add salt, butter and beaten egg yolks. Thoroughly blend. Add baking powder and stiffly beaten egg whites. Pour into a greased baking dish which will go to the table. Bake at 400 degrees for about 25 minutes or until set and browned on top. Serves 6.

Eva Easley
Bluefield, West Virginia

SLICED PEACHES

1 large can sliced peaches

Serve peaches in individual fruit bowls as a side dish. Sprinkle with nutmeg.

BAKED APPLES

4 golden delicious apples - medium size	**4 tsp butter - melted**
¼ C brown sugar - firmly packed	**½ C raisins**
	½ tsp cinnamon

Core apples and place in greased baking dish which will hold apples straight up. Mix remaining ingredients and spoon evenly into center of each apple. Bake at 350 degrees for 40 minutes. Transfer to individual serving dishes. Serve warm.

May be topped with whipped topping, ice cream or powdered sugar mixed with a small amount of milk and drizzled over. Serves 4.

HAMBURGER QUICHE

"I always double this recipe and freeze a quiche for later. Even non-quiche lovers like it."

1 unbaked 9" frozen deep
   dish pie crust
½ lb ground beef
½ C mayonnaise (Hell-
   mann's)
½ C milk
2 eggs - beaten

1 Tbsp cornstarch
¼ C chopped green pepper
¼ C chopped green onion
1½ C grated cheese (ched-
   dar and/or Swiss)
salt and pepper

Brown beef and drain. (See helpful hint # 2.) Mix mayonnaise, milk, cornstarch and eggs. Stir in meat, cheeses, onion and pepper. Season to taste. Pour into unbaked pie shell. Bake at 350 degrees for 35 - 45 minutes or until center is set. Serves 4.

CARROTS

2 C carrots - cut in julienne
   strips
4 Tbsp butter or margarine
1 tsp sugar
1 Tbsp brown sugar

1 Tbsp lemon juice
1 tsp fresh parsley
dash salt
dash nutmeg

Cook carrots then cut into strips. (See helpful hint # 17.) Melt butter in sauce pan. Combine other ingredients with butter then add carrot strips. Heat thoroughly over low heat. Serves 4.

SARAH'S SLAW

1 small <u>head cabbage</u> - shredded
2 - 3 medium <u>carrots</u> - grated
1 - 2 <u>green onion</u> and tops - finely chopped
3 Tbsp <u>sweet pickle relish</u> with vinegar
½ tsp celery seed
enough mayonnaise to hold slaw together (Hellman's)
salt and pepper to taste

Mix all ingredients and refrigerate until serving time.

"MOCK" CHEESE CAKE

1 small pkg <u>instant vanilla pudding mix</u>
1 carton (8 oz) <u>sour cream</u>
1 C milk
<u>fruit pie filling</u> - optional

<u>8" crumb Crust:</u> (bought or made)
1 C <u>graham cracker crumbs</u>
3 Tbsp melted butter

Stir crumbs and butter together. Press into bottom and part way up sides of 8" pie plate. Blend together the pudding mix and milk. Add sour cream. Pour into crust. Refrigerate. It is good plain or with your favorite fruit topping.

An old newspaper clipping,
yellow with age.

FROSTED MEAT LOAF

BROCCOLI with CHEESE WHIZ

&. **JELLIED APPLESAUCE**

DROP BISCUITS

&. **TOFFEE BARS**

FROSTED MEAT LOAF

1½ lbs ground beef - chuck
  or round
1 can golden mushroom
  soup
1 C small bread crumbs
¼ C onion - chopped fine

1 egg - beaten
½ tsp salt
pepper to taste
2 C mashed potatoes
¼ C water
1 - 2 Tbsp drippings

Thoroughly mix beef, ½ cup of undiluted soup, bread crumbs, onion, egg and seasonings. Shape into a firm loaf. (See helpful hint # 9.) Place in a shallow pan and bake at 350 degrees for 1 hour. Meanwhile prepare mashed potatoes either from scratch or instant. Remove loaf to oven-proof serving platter. *"Frost"* the loaf with mashed potatoes. Return to oven for 15 minutes longer. Combine remaining soup, water and drippings. Heat and serve with loaf. Drizzle a little over the top for decoration. Serves 6.

1968 - Cut from a magazine

BROCCOLI with CHEESE WHIZ

fresh broccoli
1 small jar Cheese Whiz

Wash and trim broccoli stalks. Drop in lightly salted boiling water for about 5 minutes. Drain and transfer to serving dish. Heat Cheese Whiz in microwave or small sauce pan over medium heat. Pour over broccoli.

JELLIED APPLESAUCE

1 pkg (3 oz) cherry gelatin
1 C canned apple sauce

Dissolve gelatin in 1 C boiling water. Add 1 C applesauce.
Refrigerate until firm. Serves 4.

DROP BICUITS

1½ - 2 C biscuit mix

Prepare biscuit mix according to package directions. Have
dough on *"wet"* side. Drop by rounded tablespoons onto greased
baking sheet. Bake at 425 degrees until golden brown - about 12
- 15 minutes.

TOFFEE BARS

1 stick butter - softened
1 stick margarine - softened
1 C brown sugar - firmly packed
1 egg yolk
dash salt
2 C flour
½ tsp vanilla extract
1 (6 oz) pkg chocolate morsels - melted
1 C chopped pecans

Cream margarine and butter with brown sugar. Add egg yolk,
salt, flour and vanilla. Blend well. Press into an ungreased 9 x 11
inch pan. Bake at 350 degrees for 15 - 20 minutes. Cool slightly
then spread with melted chocolate morsels and sprinkle with
chopped nuts. Cool completely before cutting into squares. Pass
around the table.

BRUNSWICK STEW

2 - 3 lb whole chicken with giblets
3 - 4 medium carrots - sliced
1 medium yellow onion - sliced
3 - 4 ribs celery - chopped
1 one pound can whole tomatoes
1 can (8 oz) tomato sauce
1 poly - bag frozen baby limas
1 poly - bag frozen corn or 2 cans (drained)
1 box frozen green peas
3 medium size white potatoes - diced
1 Tbsp salt
1 Tbsp sugar (do not omit)
1 tsp pepper
few drops hot sauce

Cover chicken and giblets in large pot with lightly salted water. Boil until chicken is well done and falls from the bone. Meantime, chop the raw vegetables. Remove chicken from broth and chop fine. Discard giblets. Strain broth into soup kettle. Add water or canned broth to make 6 cups. Cook raw vegetables in broth. When vegetables are tender, remove about 2 cups and mash with a potato masher (this helps thicken stew). Add frozen vegetables and chicken to broth and continue to cook. Stir occasionally to prevent scorching. Add mashed vegetables back to stew. (See helpful hint # 6.) Correct seasoning. Parsley may be added. (See helpful hint # 25.) Simmer at least 30 minutes longer. This is better if made a day ahead. This makes a big pot of stew. Freezes well.

FRESH GREEN SALAD

Toss a green salad with your favorite dressing. A blue cheese dressing is especially good with this meal.

SAUSAGE PINWHEELS

1 lb hot bulk sausage - cooked, crumbled and drained prepared biscuit mix

Prepare biscuit dough with 2 - 2½ cups mix. Roll dough on floured surface in rectangular shape. Spread cooked sausage over dough. Roll up like a jelly roll and slice about ¾ inch thick. Place slices with sides touching on greased jelly-roll pan. Bake at 400 degrees for 12 - 15 minutes or until brown. Serves 6.

RAW APPLE CAKE

"This cake is great at Christmas time. I make two "batches" while I have everything out and freeze for Christmas gifts."

2 C sugar
1½ C oil
3 eggs
3 C flour
1 tsp cinnamon
1 tsp salt
1 tsp soda
1 tsp vanilla
1 C chopped dates
2 C shredded coconut
3 C raw golden delicious apples - peeled and diced
1 C chopped pecans

Cream sugar and oil. Add eggs one at a time. Beat well. Combine flour, cinnamon, salt and soda. Gradually add to egg mixture. Mix well. Stir in vanilla, coconut, dates, apples and nuts. Batter will be thick. Pour into a greased and floured tube pan or 2 - 3 loaf pans (depending on size). Bake at 325 degrees for 1½ hours. Allow to cool in pan until cool enough to touch.

Mother, Elizabeth F. Easley
Danville, Virginia

SAUSAGE and WILD RICE

1 box Uncle Ben's long grain and wild rice
1 lb bulk sausage
1 can mushroom stems and pieces or 6-8 large fresh

Prepare rice as package directs. Cook sausage, drain and crumble. If fresh mushrooms are used, slice and sauté in pan drippings or drain canned mushrooms. Add all together and place in greased casserole. Heat in 350 degree oven for about 20 minutes or until thoroughly heated. Serves 6.

"Children love this and it is a quick casserole to take to a neighbor in need."

Betty Rose T. Sexton

RAW VEGETABLE SALAD

mushrooms - small whole buttons
cucumber - thinly sliced
broccoli - small flowerettes
cauliflower - small flowerettes
carrots - thinly sliced
onion - thinly sliced rings
oil and vinegar salad dressing

Prepare vegetables. Pour oil and vinegar dressing over and refrigerate in a container with a tight fitting lid. At serving time shake to re-mix. Remove vegetables with slotted spoon to salad bowl.

SIX-WEEK MUFFINS

1 box (10 oz) <u>raisin bran cereal</u>
1 C vegetable shortening - melted
3 C sugar
4 eggs - beaten
1 qt <u>buttermilk</u>
5 C self-rising flour
5 tsp soda
5 tsp salt

In a large bowl mix bran, sugar, flour, soda and salt. Add eggs, melted shortening and milk. Mix well. Fill greased muffin tins ⅔ full. Bake at 400 degrees for 15 - 20 minutes. Store remaining batter in a covered container in refrigerator. Will keep up to 6 weeks and improves with age. These muffins are wonderful for breakfast, too.

1978 - Jane Wootton

APPLE SPICE BARS

½ C butter or margarine
⅓ C firmly packed brown sugar
1 C white sugar
1 egg
¼ C milk
½ tsp vanilla
½ C <u>nuts</u> (optional)
2 <u>apples</u> - peeled and chopped fine
2 C flour
1 tsp soda
1 tsp cinnamon
½ tsp nutmeg
½ tsp salt
dash allspice
1 C <u>golden raisins</u>

Cream butter and sugars. Add egg and beat well. Sift flour and spices together. Combine all ingredients. Spread in a greased jelly-roll pan. Bake at 350 degrees for 10 - 15 minutes. Cool then cut into rectangles. Cookies are soft.

Anne M. Grigg

SHRIMP CREOLE
CHEESE RICE
QUICK LITTLE LOAF BREAD
TOSSED SALAD
LEMON COOKIES

SHRIMP CREOLE

Combine in a large skillet or dutch oven:
½ C <u>olive oil</u>
½ C <u>chopped bacon</u> - cut with scissors

2 cloves <u>garlic</u> - minced
⅔ C <u>celery</u> - chopped
1 large onion - chopped
1 medium <u>green pepper</u> - chopped

Cook over medium heat until bacon and onion are clear.

Add the following to the above mixture:
1 large <u>can tomatoes</u>
2 cans (6 oz) <u>tomato paste</u>
1 C water
1½ tsp sugar
2 tsp Worcestershire
½ tsp <u>tabasco</u>
salt and pepper to taste

Simmer this sauce for about 3 hours. May be made a day ahead or frozen. Also may cook in a crock pot 6 - 8 hours. Either way, cook until thickened, stirring occasionally.

About 10 - 15 minutes before serving time add:
2½ lbs <u>shrimp</u> - cleaned raw or frozen and thawed

Continue to cook for 10 - 15 minutes longer or until shrimp are cooked and thoroughly heated. Serve with cheese rice. Serves 6-8.

"The best"
Jane Wootton

40

CHEESE RICE

1 onion - chopped very fine
rice - 2 - 3 C cooked
1 C sharp cheddar cheese - grated
salt

Cook onion in water in which rice is to be cooked. Cook enough rice to yield about 2 - 3 cups cooked. Stir grated cheese into cooked rice until melted. Make a ring of rice on a large serving platter and place shrimp creole in the center.

Jane Wootton

QUICK LITTLE LOAF BREAD

¼ C vegetable shortening
¼ C sugar
3 eggs - beaten
2 C flour
2½ tsp baking powder
1 tsp salt
1 C milk

In mixer bowl at medium speed, cream shortening and sugar. Add eggs one at a time. Combine dry ingredients and add alternately with milk beginning and ending with flour. Do not overbeat. Batter may be lumpy. Pour into greased loaf pan. Bake at 350 degrees for 45 - 50 minutes.

LEMON COOKIES

"Pass a plate of cookies around the table for dessert."

1 pkg lemon cake mix (Duncan Hines)
2 C Cool Whip (4½ oz) - thawed
1 egg
½ - 1 C powdered sugar

Mix cake mix, whipped topping and egg in large bowl of electric mixer until smooth. Batter will be thick. Place powdered sugar in large flat dish. Drop batter by teaspoonsful into sugar and roll to coat. Place cookies on greased cookie sheet. Flatten slightly. Bake at 350 degrees for about 15 minutes. Cool on wire rack. Makes about 4 - 5 dozen.

BEEF BURGUNDY

1½ - 2 lbs <u>round steak</u> - sliced in thin strips
1 medium <u>onion</u> - sliced thin
2 Tbsp oil
2 Tbsp flour
½ tsp thyme
½ tsp <u>marjoram</u>
salt and pepper to taste
1 C <u>beef bouillon</u> - canned
2 C <u>dry burgundy wine</u>
½ lb <u>fresh mushrooms</u> - sliced

In an electric skillet or dutch oven, cook the onion in oil until transparent. Set aside. Add beef to oil (use more if needed) and brown. Sprinkle flour over beef while cooking. Drain off excess oil if necessary. Add herbs and seasonings. Stir in bouillon and wine. Cover and simmer stirring occasionally, for 1 - 1½ hours or place dutch oven in a 350 degree oven for 1 - 1½ hours. Keep meat barely covered with liquid. If more is needed add in a ratio of 2 parts wine to 1 part bouillon. (If children do not like wine, use all bouillon). Add onions and fresh mushrooms for the last half hour of cooking time. Serve over rice. Serves 6.

RICE

Cook rice according to package directions. A Tbsp of instant bouillon added to the rice water adds extra flavor.

BROILED TOMATOES

medium sized tomatoes

Cut tops from tomatoes and stand in muffin tins. Place a thin pat of butter on top then sprinkle with salt and pepper, dried oregano and parmesan cheese. Bake in 350 degree oven for 15 minutes and then under broiler for 1 - 2 minutes until cheese begins to brown.

SLICED LETTUCE SALAD

crisp lettuce
purple onion - sliced in rings
green pepper - sliced in rings
your favorite salad dressing

Slice head of lettuce about ¾ inches thick and place circle on salad plate. Garnish with onion and pepper rings. Top with your favorite salad dressing.

CRESCENT ROLLS - Bake refrigerator crescents as package directs.

DATE-NUT BARS

2 sticks butter
1 lb chopped dates
1⅓ C sugar
4 C Rice Krispies
3 C chopped pecans
2 tsp vanilla

In a heavy sauce pan combine butter, dates and sugar. Over medium high heat boil exactly 5 minutes from time of first few bubbles. Stir to keep from sticking. Remove from heat. Add vanilla and pour over Rice Krispies and pecans in a large bowl. Mix well. Smooth into a 9 x 13" pan. Dust with powdered sugar. (See helpful hint # 33.) Cut into small squares.

Fitz's favorite since Christmas 1983

SWEET AND SOUR BEEF CHUNKS

RICE

BROCCOLI

BEER BREAD

CHOCOLATE CHESS PIE

SWEET AND SOUR BEEF

1½ - 2 lbs round steak - cubed
2 Tbsp oil
2 Tbsp flour
½ tsp salt
1 large can tomatoes
⅓ C brown sugar
⅓ C cider vinegar
1 medium onion - sliced
1 small green pepper - sliced

Cook onion in oil until clear. Reserve. Add beef to oil and brown. Sprinkle flour over beef when nearly all red is gone. Drain excess fat if necessary. Place in dutch oven or casserole with tight fitting lid. Add all remaining ingredients except green pepper. Cook in a 350 degree oven for 1 - 1½ hours until meat is tender and mixture is thickened. Cut pepper into thick strips and add during last 15 - 20 minutes of cooking time. This dish may be made several days in advance and kept in refrigerator. This improves flavor. Do not recommend freezing. Serves 6.

1967 - Ruth Plieter
Baltimore, Maryland

Rice - Cook rice as package directs.

BROCCOLI

1 - 2 bunches <u>fresh broccoli</u>
<u>green goddess dressing</u>

Wash and trim broccoli flowerettes. Place in individual bowls with green goddess dressing. Serve like a dip.

BEER BREAD

3 C <u>whole wheat flour</u>
1 tsp baking powder
1 tsp baking soda
2 Tbsp <u>honey</u>
1 tsp salt
12 oz <u>dark beer or stout</u>

Put dry ingredients in a bowl. Add honey. Pour in beer, stirring with a spoon only until moistened. Place in a greased loaf pan. Bake at 350 degrees for 45 - 55 minutes or until loaf sounds hollow when thumped. Remove from pan and brush top of loaf with melted butter. Slice and serve hot with lots of butter.

Cary Wineholtz

CHOCOLATE CHESS PIE

1 <u>unbaked pie crust</u>

½ stick margarine
1½ squares <u>unsweetened chocolate</u>
1½ C sugar
1 Tbsp flour
2 eggs
½ C milk
1 tsp vanilla
pinch salt

Melt margarine and chocolate together. Stir in sugar. Combine all remaining ingredients and add chocolate mixture. Pour into unbaked crust. Bake at 350 degrees for 30 - 40 minutes. Top will be crusty. Serve with whipped topping.

1965 - Mrs. A.A. Farley
Danville, Virginia

SARAH'S SHRIMP

large shrimp with tails - I use frozen
1 stick butter or margarine
1 lemon - juiced
1 lemon - cut in wedges

Thaw shrimp on paper towel. Allow 6 - 8 shrimp per adult. Melt butter in skillet. Sauté shrimp. Remove to serving platter. Add lemon juice to butter then drizzle over shrimp. May garnish with parsley. Serve immediately with lemon wedges.

SPEEDY SPINACH

2 boxes frozen chopped spinach
1 package (1 ⅜ oz) dry onion soup mix
1 pt sour cream
salt and pepper to taste

Place frozen spinach in large sauce pan over low heat. Add NO water. Cover and watch closely until spinach is thawed and cooked about 10 minutes. Remove from heat. Drain. Add soup mix, sour cream and seasonings. Place mixture in a greased casserole and bake at 300 degrees for 30 minutes. May make ahead. Keeps well in refrigerator. Serves 6 - 8.

NOODLES

medium flat noodles
butter
parmesan cheese

Cook noodles in large pot in lots of water. Drain. Toss with butter, salt and parmesan cheese. Basil or parsley may be added for extra flavor and color.

CORN MUFFINS

1 C corn meal
2 tsp baking powder
1 tsp salt
1 egg
1 C buttermilk

Beat egg and milk together. (See helpful hint # 15.) Mix dry ingredients and add to milk. Stir with a spoon. Batter will be thick. Spoon into greased muffin tins. Bake at 425 degrees for 15 - 20 minutes.

LEMON PIE

1 9" unbaked pie shell
1 lemon - thin skin
1 ¼ C sugar
1 stick margarine - cut into chunks
4 eggs
dash salt

Cut lemon in wedges. Remove seeds and center membrane. Place all ingredients in the blender and turn on "high" for 1½ minutes by the clock. Pour into an unbaked pie shell. Bake at 350 degrees for about 30 minutes or until set.

Janet Coleman

MARINATED PORK ROAST

BROCCOLI CASSEROLE

HOT PEACHES

BISCUITS

CHERRY CRUNCH

MARINATED PORK ROAST

4 - 5 lb pork loin roast - boned, rolled and tied

MARINADE:

2 Tbsp dry mustard	**2 cloves of garlic**
2 tsp dry thyme	**½ C sherry**
1 tsp ground ginger	**½ C soy sauce**

Mix ingredients and pour over roast. Marinate roast at least 4 hours or day ahead. Turn occasionally. (See helpful hint # 22.) Place roast in open roasting pan on a rack. Roast at 350 degrees for 30 - 35 minutes per pound. Set timer on oven if needed. Allow roast to stand 5 minutes before carving. Serve with apricot sauce. Serves 6.

APRICOT SAUCE:

1 jar apricot preserves	**1 Tbsp sherry**
1 Tbsp soy sauce	

Heat in sauce pan. Serve in a sauce boat.

Martha F. Ray
Danville, Virginia

HOT PEACHES

1 can peach halves
1 small jar mincemeat pie filling - or raisins

Place peaches with juice in greased baking dish. Sprinkle with cinnamon and fill the center with pie filling. Heat in 350 degree oven for 15 - 20 minutes. If raisins are used, cook in the juice then spoon into peach half at serving time.

1980 - Jane P. Wootton

BROCCOLI CASSEROLE

2 pkg frozen chopped broccoli - thawed
1 stick margarine - melted
1 can mushroom soup
1 can (8 oz) mushrooms with liquid
½ C onion - chopped
½ C celery - chopped
1 C minute rice - uncooked
½ C water
1 small jar Cheeze Whiz

Mix all ingredients and put in a sprayed casserole. Bake at 350 degrees for 25 - 30 minutes. Serves 6 - 8.

Martha F. Ray
Danville, Virginia

BISCUITS

2 C biscuit mix
1 pkg dry yeast
½ C warm water (105 degrees)

Mix yeast with warm water and allow to stand until dissolved. In large bowl stir water into biscuit mix. More water may be added. Mix well. Roll out biscuits on floured surface. Cut and bake at 450 degrees until brown - about 10 - 15 minutes. Makes about a dozen.

CHERRY CRUNCH

1 can cherry pie filling
1 small box yellow cake mix (1 layer size)
½ C pecans
¼ C sugar
½ C margarine

Pour pie filling into greased baking dish. Cut margarine into cake mix with pastry blender. Add sugar and pecans. Mixture resembles coarse corn meal. Sprinkle over pie filling. Bake at 350 degrees for 45 minutes until golden brown and "crunchy" on top.

HERBED CHICKEN

1 C plain <u>bread crumbs</u>
½ C grated parmesan
   cheese
¼ tsp fresh ground pepper
½ tsp oregano
¾ tsp basil
¾ tsp thyme
½ tsp salt
⅔ C margarine - melted
4 - 6 <u>chicken breasts</u> -
   boned and skinned

Combine bread crumbs, (See helpful hint # 9.) cheese, herbs and seasonings in plastic bag. Dip chicken pieces into melted butter then shake in bag with crumb mixture. Coat well. Place chicken in greased baking dish. Bake at 350 degrees for 1 hour. Serves 4 - 6.

SARAH'S POTATO BAKE

2 C <u>instant mashed potatoes</u>
2 Tbsp margarine - melted
½ C <u>sour cream</u>
1 - 2 Tbsp <u>chives</u> - chopped
salt and pepper to taste
½ C <u>sharp cheese</u> - grated

Make 2 cups of instant mashed potatoes using a little less milk so as to have potatoes on "dry" side. Add 2 additional tablespoons of melted margarine, ½ cup sour cream, chopped chives and salt and pepper. Place in a sprayed casserole. Top with grated cheese. Heat in a 350 degree oven for about 15 - 20 minutes until thoroughly hot and cheese melts. Serves 4 - 6.

<u>GREEN PEAS</u> - Your favorite canned or frozen.

BLUEBERRY SALAD

1 pkg (6 oz) <u>black cherry</u>
  <u>gelatin</u>
2 C hot water
1 can (15 oz) <u>blueberries -</u>
  <u>drained</u>

1 can (8¼ oz) <u>crushed</u>
  <u>pineapple</u> - undrained
1 envelope <u>plain gelatin</u>

Add hot water to cherry gelatin. Stir until dissolved. Sprinkle unflavored gelatin on small amount of pineapple juice and allow to stand until soft. Combine all ingredients. Pour into 13 x 9 x 2-inch pan. Chill until firm.

TOPPING:

1 (8 oz) pkg <u>cream cheese -</u>
  softened
1 (8 oz) carton <u>sour cream</u>

½ C sugar
½ C <u>chopped walnuts</u>

Combine cream cheese, sour cream and sugar until smooth. Add walnuts. Spread on top of congealed mixture. Cut in squares and serve on lettuce leaf.

Mother, Elizabeth F. Easley
Danville, Virginia

SCOTCH SHORTBREAD

"This is especially good to have on hand during the holidays."

2 sticks <u>butter</u> - no substitute
1½ C <u>flour</u> - measure before sifting

¾ C <u>corn starch</u>
¾ C <u>powdered sugar</u>
aluminum foil

Soften butter - may partially melt. Sift dry ingredients together into large bowl of electric mixer. Add butter at low speed. Batter will be stiff. Knead remaining flour mixture in by hand if batter becomes too heavy for mixer. Pat into a foil lined 7 x 11 inch pan. Prick top with a fork. Bake at 340 degrees for 30 minutes. Will brown as it cools. Sprinkle with granulated sugar and cut while hot. Allow to cool in pan. Store in a very tightly covered tin. Keeps well. Recipe may be doubled.

Jane P. Wootton
December 1972

CHICKEN POT PIE

TOSSED SALAD

❧ **CHOCOLATE CHIP CAKE**

CHICKEN POT PIE

1 Tbsp cooking oil
1½ lbs boneless chicken breasts
1 pkg (2.4 oz) Knorr leek soup mix
1½ Tbsp flour
3 C water
3 medium white potatoes - cubed
2 medium carrots - cut up
1 pkg frozen peas
1 pkg refrigerator crescent rolls

In a large dutch oven, heat oil over high heat. Cut chicken into 1 inch pieces and brown on all sides in oil. Remove chicken. Quickly stir in soup mix and flour. Stir in water. Bring to a boil, stirring constantly. Add chicken, potatoes and carrots. Reduce heat and cook about 15 minutes until vegetables are fork tender and mixture has thickened. Add peas. Turn into a large baking dish (11 x 7 x 2) and cover top with a single layer of crescent roll dough. Bake at 350 degrees for about 15 minutes or until top is golden brown. Serves 6.

A Knorr Recipe

TOSSED SALAD

Have a hearty salad using a variety of greens and raw vegetables. Add chilled water chestnuts to salad for an extra crunch. A blue cheese or French dressing is especially good.

CHOCOLATE CHIP CAKE

"One of our most favorites."

1 box marble cake mix (Duncan Hines)
1 box instant vanilla pudding mix
½ C oil
1 C water
4 eggs
8 - 10 oz chocolate chips

In a large mixing bowl mix together the white packet mix, pudding mix, oil, water and eggs. Mix well. In a small mixing bowl mix the chocolate packet mix and 1½ cups of the white batter. Stir the chocolate chips into the remaining white batter. Grease and flour a tube pan. Pour white batter with chocolate chips into pan first. Pour chocolate batter on top and knife it in to swirl. Bake at 350 degrees for 45 - 60 minutes. Cool completely before removing from pan. Serve with frozen whipped topping or just pass around a plate of slices.

Betty Rose T. Sexton
September 1984

NOTES

NOTES

SPRING

SPRING

MAIN DISHES

Butterflied Leg-O-Lamb • Whole Leg of Lamb • Lamb Curry • Eye of Round Roast • Sour Cream Baked Cod • Lemon Chicken • Beth's Chicken Dijon • Barbecued Chicken • Margaret's Chicken • First Warm Day Picnic • Breaded Soft Shell Crabs • Crabmeat Casserole • Shad Roe • Crab Cakes • Marinated London Broil • Sautéed Veal and Fresh Mushrooms • Marinated Flank Steak • Salmon Loaf with Horseradish Sauce • Barbecued Spareribs • Sweet and Sour Pork

VEGETABLES

Fresh Green Beans • Zesty Carrots • Mashed Sweet Potatoes • Broccoli with Lemon Butter • Rice • Buttered Peas and Carrots • Baked Potato • Asparagus • Cheese Grits • Baby Lima Beans • Stewed Corn • Vegetable Casserole • Broiled Tomatoes • Rice Pilaf • Cottage Fries • Stuffed Tomatoes • Spinach and Cheese • Great Potato Casserole • Fettuccini • Green Pea Casserole • New Red Potatoes • Potato Bake • Snow Pea Pods

SALADS

Bing Cherry • Lettuce Wedges • Tossed • Pear • Bean • Crudite • Cole Slaw • 24-Hour Slaw • Vegetable Medley • Fresh Spinach

BREADS

Bakery Loaf • Herb Bread • Easy Loaf Bread • Lemon Loaf • Refrigerator Bread Sticks • Jane's Batter Bread • Rosemary Rolls • Corn Bread • Crescent Roll-Ups with Ham • Corn Spoonbread • Griddle Cakes • Cheese Bread • Beer Muffins • Light Muffins • Lacy Griddle Cakes

DESSERTS

Chocolate Squares • Fresh Strawberries • Pudding and Berries • Lemon Bars • Chocolate Pie • Lemon Loaf • Lemon Ice-Box Pie • Fresh Strawberry Pie • Angel Food Cake Dessert • Fresh Fruit and Cheese • Strawberry Trifle • Strawberry Shortcake • Carolyn's Cookies • Pound Cake • Eclairs • Ice Cream Pie • Coconut Pound Cake • No-Crust Coconut Pie • Chocolate Sundae • Ladyfinger Layer Cake

SPRING

🦪 BUTTERFLIED LEG - O - LAMB - GRILLED

FRESH GREEN BEANS

ZESTY CARROTS

BAKERY LOAF

CHOCOLATE SQUARES

BUTTERFLIED LEG - O - LAMB - GRILLED

1 whole leg of lamb - butterflied
Dijon mustard

green onions
dried oregano

Have a butcher butterfly a leg of lamb. Use only half a leg for fewer people. (This is not good left over.) Remove skin and most of fat. Open meat with skin side down. Spread generously with Dijon mustard. Sprinkle with chopped green onions, oregano, salt and pepper. Tie meat in "flat" roll. Grill over medium hot coals for at least 1 hour. Turn and baste every 15 minutes. Close grill top or cover meat with large inverted roasting pan. Whole leg serves 8 - 10. Half a leg serves 4.

BASTING SAUCE

6 Tbsp melted butter
2 tsp dried oregano
1 tsp onion juice or grated
  onion

1 Tbsp Worcestershire
1 Tbsp soy sauce

Serve remaining basting sauce with meat. (See helpful hint # 37.)

FRESH GREEN BEANS

fresh new green beans
oil and vinegar salad dressing

Wash and trim green beans. Blanch in boiling water for about 2 - 3 minutes. Pour off hot water and immediately cover in cold water to stop cooking process. Drain. Pour salad dressing over beans and marinate in the refrigerator until serving time.

ZESTY CARROTS

6 - 8 large <u>carrots</u>
2 Tbsp grated onion
2 Tbsp <u>horseradish</u> (do not reduce)
½ C mayonnaise (Hellmann's)
½ tsp salt
¼ tsp pepper
¼ C bread crumbs
1 Tbsp butter

Peel carrots. Cook whole in salted water just until tender. (See helpful hint # 17.) Drain. Cut into julienne strips. Arrange in a sprayed shallow baking dish. Mix remaining ingredients and pour over carrots. Top with buttered bread crumbs. (See helpful hint # 9.) Bake at 375 degrees for 15 - 20 minutes. Serves 6.

Margie Ayres

BAKERY LOAF BREAD

Slice <u>loaf of bakery bread</u> and butter. Wrap in aluminum foil. Heat in oven. Peel back foil and serve.

CHOCOLATE SQUARES

"A chocolate lover's cookie."

2 C <u>graham cracker crumbs</u>
12 oz <u>chocolate chips</u>
1 can <u>sweetened condensed milk</u>

Mix all ingredients together. Place in a greased oblong pan. Bake at 350 degrees for 20 minutes. Cool before cutting into squares. This is great to pass around at the cookout.

WHOLE LEG of LAMB

whole leg of lamb - **skinned**
ground oregano
mint jelly

Wash lamb and pat dry. Be sure all skin is cut away. Rub ground oregano over outside. Place leg on a rack in a greased roasting pan. Cover bottom of pan with water. Preheat oven to 450 degrees. Put lamb in oven and turn immediately to 350 degrees. Roast 20 minutes per pound. Lamb is much more flavorful if slightly rare. Make gravy of pan drippings. Serve with mint jelly. Serves 8 - 10.

MASHED SWEET POTATOES

3 large sweet potatoes	**dash salt**
½ C brown sugar	**dash nutmeg**
6 Tbsp butter or margarine	**mini marshmallows**
1 orange - juice and zest	

Cover potatoes in water and boil until tender. Peel and coarsely cut into large bowl of electric mixer. Beat at medium speed until smooth. Add brown sugar - more if desired, butter - melt if potatoes have cooled, the orange (See helpful hint # 13.) and seasonings. Smooth into a greased casserole. Place in a 350 degree oven until thoroughly heated, then add marshmallows and return to oven for 5 - 10 minutes or until marshmallows have browned. Watch closely. Serves 6 - 8.

BROCCOLI - 3 bunches <u>fresh broccoli</u>. Cut off stalk. Steam flowerettes over boiling water for about 5 minutes. Mix the juice of one lemon and 4 Tbsp melted butter. Pour over broccoli. Salt to taste. Serve immediately. Serves 6.

BING CHERRY SALAD

1 small box <u>dark cherry gelatin</u>
1 can pitted <u>bing cherries</u> - drained
1 small can <u>crushed pineapple</u> - drained
½ C <u>slivered almonds</u>
½ envelope unflavored gelatin
1 small package <u>cream cheese</u>
¼ C <u>orange marmalade</u>

Use drained juices with water to make 2 cups liquid. Heat 1 cup juice and mix with gelatin. Sprinkle unflavored gelatin over second cup and allow to stand until dissolved. Combine the juices, then add the fruit. Refrigerate until firm. Make topping by stirring together softened cream cheese and marmalade. Spoon a dollop of topping on each serving. Serves 8.

ROLLS - Purchase dinner <u>rolls</u> from the bakery.

STRAWBERRIES

fresh <u>strawberries</u>
<u>frozen whipped topping</u> or whipped cream

Wash and cap strawberries. Sprinkle with powdered sugar and refrigerate during dinner. Stir as little as possible. Top individual servings with a large spoon of whipped topping. If whipped cream is preferred: Beat until stiff and sweeten with powdered sugar.

LAMB CURRY with CONDIMENTS

3 C cooked lamb - finely chopped
1 can beef bouillon
½ C celery - diced
½ C onion - chopped
5 Tbsp margarine - divided
3 Tbsp flour
1 tsp curry powder
salt to taste

In a large sauce pan melt 2 Tbsp margarine. Sauté onions and celery. Remove with slotted spoon. Add remaining margarine and melt. Blend in flour until smooth. Add beef bouillon. Stir until well blended and thickened. Add cooked lamb (this is a good way to use left-over lamb), onion, celery, curry and salt. Simmer about 15 - 20 minutes or longer, stirring occasionally. Add more bouillon if it gets too thick. Serve over rice. Serves 4.

Have small bowls of condiments to accompany curry.

CONDIMENTS:
   chopped peanuts
   grated coconut
   chutney
   crushed pineapple - drained
   raisins
   chopped banana

RICE

Cook white rice as package directs to yield 2 - 3 C of cooked rice.

BUTTERED PEAS and CARROTS

1 box frozen green peas
2 C cut - up carrots
1 Tbsp honey
2 Tbsp butter
parsley flakes

Slice carrots. Drop peas and carrots into rapidly boiling salted water for 5 - 7 minutes. Drain. Toss lightly with butter and honey. Salt to taste and sprinkle with parsley flakes - dried or fresh. Serves 4.

SOUR DOUGH ROLLS - Purchase from bakery

PUDDING and BERRIES

1 box instant vanilla pudding mix
1 C milk
1 C frozen whipped topping - thawed
fresh strawberries
1 pkg ladyfingers

Add milk to pudding mix and stir until smooth. Fold in whipped topping. Arrange split ladyfingers around a fruit bowl or sherbet dish. Wash, hull and slice strawberries reserving one whole berry for the top of each serving. Strawberries may be sprinkled lightly with powdered sugar if desired. Spoon strawberries over ladyfingers then spoon pudding mixture over all. Top with a whole strawberry. Refrigerate until serving time.

ʕ❦ EYE of ROUND ROAST

BAKED POTATO

ASPARAGUS

LETTUCE WEDGES

HERB BREAD

ʕ❦ LEMON BARS

EYE of ROUND ROAST

eye of round roast
1 bottle of French dressing
1 Tbsp oregano

Wash roast and pat dry. Place roast on large piece of aluminum foil. Rub with oregano and pour French dressing over. Wrap tightly in foil. Roast about 20 - 25 minutes per pound at 350 degrees. Preparation may be done early and oven timer set. When done, place on serving platter, slice and pour gravy over.

BAKED POTATO - One baking potato per person. Wash, dry with paper towel, prick skin with a fork and rub with bacon drippings. Bake in 350 degree oven for 1 hour or until soft to touch. Serve with butter, sour cream mixed with chives and grated cheese.

ASPARAGUS

Select small asparagus, slightly larger than a pencil. Wash and cut off whitish ends. Bind asparagus with a narrow strip of aluminum foil so they will stand straight up. Stand in a sauce pan with 1 - 1½ inches boiling water. Cover and cook about 5 minutes. Remove from water, drain, and place in flat serving dish. Pour melted butter over and salt to taste.

64

LETTUCE WEDGES

1 head <u>lettuce</u> - firm
<u>thousand island dressing</u>

Peel loose outer leaves from lettuce and reserve. Cut whole head into wedges and top with thousand island dressing.

HERB BREAD

2 C <u>biscuit mix</u>	½ C milk
1 Tbsp sugar	¼ C margarine - melted
2 tsp dried onion flakes	¼ C <u>dry white wine</u>
½ tsp oregano	⅓ C parmesan cheese -
1 egg - beaten	divided

Combine dry ingredients. Using a spoon, stir in liquids and beaten egg. Add all but 2 Tbsp of the parmesan cheese. Pour into a greased round casserole. Sprinkle reserved parmesan cheese on top. Bake at 400 degrees for 25 minutes. Transfer to serving plate and cut in wedges at the table.

LEMON BARS

½ C soft butter - do not substitute	1 C flour
	¼ C powdered sugar

Cut butter into flour and sugar with a pastry blender. Pat into a greased oblong pan. Bake 15 - 20 minutes at 325 degrees. Crust is firm and beginning to brown at edges.

FILLING:

2 eggs - beaten well	1 C sugar
3 Tbsp <u>lemon juice</u>	2 Tbsp flour
1½ tsp grated <u>lemon rind</u>	

Combine filling ingredients (See helpful hint # 13.) When crust is removed from oven immediately pour filling over. Return to oven for 20 minutes longer. Sprinkle with powdered sugar. Cool in the pan before cutting.

SOUR CREAM BAKED COD

2 lbs cod fillets (or flounder)
1 Tbsp vegetable oil (do
not increase)
½ C fine dry bread crumbs
1 C sour cream
1 Tbsp fresh parsley -
chopped

1 Tbsp green onion -
chopped
1 tsp lemon juice
½ tsp salt
⅛ tsp pepper
¼ C milk
⅓ C parmesan cheese
½ tsp paprika

Pour oil into baking dish. Heat in a 400 degree oven for 5 minutes. Pat fish dry with paper towels. Combine bread crumbs, sour cream, parsley, onion, lemon juice, salt, pepper and milk. Arrange fish in a single layer in the hot dish. Spread sour cream mixture over fish. Sprinkle with parmesan cheese and paprika. Bake at 400 degrees for 15 - 20 minutes or until fish is flaky. Serve with lemon wedges. Serves 6 - 8.

Beth Fosdal
Middleton, Wisconsin

CHEESE GRITS

1 C grits
1 stick margarine
2 C grated sharp cheese
2 eggs - beaten

½ C milk
dash cayenne pepper
salt to taste

Cook 1 cup grits according to package directions. Add remaining ingredients to cooked grits. Pour into a greased oblong baking dish. Bake at 350 degrees for 1 hour. Serves 6.

Louise C. Mondy

66

TOSSED GREEN SALAD with VINEGARETTE

A combination of fresh greens and vegetables. Toss with a light **VINEGARETTE:** ½ cup herb or white wine vinegar, 1½ C vegetable oil, 1½ tsp salt and ¾ tsp white pepper. Dissolve salt and pepper in vinegar. Add oil and shake vigorously. Store in covered jar in refrigerator.

EASY LOAF BREAD

2 C Bisquick
¾ C milk
soft butter
1 tsp dried basil
onion salt

Combine Bisquick and milk. Roll out in a rectangle ¼" thick on a floured surface. Spread with butter. Sprinkle with basil and onion salt. Roll up jelly - roll fashion. Place on a greased cookie sheet or in a long loaf pan. Cut ⅓ way through loaf at 1 inch intervals to make slices. Bake at 450 degrees for about 20 minutes

CHOCOLATE PIE

1 chocolate crumb crust (bought or made)
1 6 oz pkg chocolate bits
2 Tbsp strong coffee
1 tsp vanilla
1 egg
2 Tbsp sugar
dash salt
¾ C boiling water
whipped topping - optional

Place all ingredients in the blender and blend on high for 1 minute. Pour into crumb crust and refrigerate 1 hour until set. Top with whipped topping.

Janet Coleman

SPRING

LEMON CHICKEN

4 - 6 chicken breasts - skinned and boned
flour for dredging
vegetable oil
2 green onion tops - chopped
1 lemon - juiced
1 Tbsp instant chicken bouillon
fresh parsley - optional

Wash chicken breasts and pat dry. On a cutting board, pound with a meat hammer until flat and about ¼ inch thickness. Dredge in flour. Brown in oil over medium high heat. Remove chicken to paper towel. Pour remaining oil from pan. Mix bouillon with 1 cup hot water. Stir to dissolve. Pour small amount of bouillon into pan. Add onions and cook for about a minute. Add chicken. Squeeze lemon juice over chicken then add remaining bouillon. Cover and simmer until sauce is slightly thickened - 5 to 10 minutes. Transfer to a serving platter. Spoon sauce over and garnish with fresh parsley sprigs. Serves 4 - 6.

BABY LIMA BEANS

frozen baby lima beans
butter or margarine

Drop frozen beans into lightly salted boiling water. Simmer about 45 minutes. Drain. Add butter and salt to taste.

STEWED CORN

cut kernel corn - canned or frozen
bacon drippings

Heat corn in lightly salted water for 20 - 30 minutes. Add generous teaspoon of bacon drippings and salt to taste.

If there are left - over beans and corn, combine as succotach for another meal. May be frozen. (See helpful hints # 3 and # 12.)

PEAR SALAD

canned pear halves
mayonnaise
grated cheddar cheese

Arrange pear halves on bed of lettuce. Dollop mayonnaise in center and sprinkle with grated cheese.

LEMON LOAF

"This bread is so good, I pass it around again for dessert."

½ C margarine - softened
1¼ C sugar - divided
2 eggs
1½ C flour
½ tsp salt
1 tsp baking powder
½ C milk
1 whole lemon - grated rind and juice

Cream margarine with 1 cup sugar until fluffy. Add eggs one at a time and beat well. Sift dry ingredients and add in thirds to creamed mixture alternating with milk. Stir in grated lemon rind (See helpful hint # 13.) and about 1 Tbsp lemon juice. Pour into a greased and floured loaf pan. Bake at 325 degrees for 1 hour. Combine remaining lemon juice and ¼ cup sugar. Heat to dissolve. Spoon over loaf when removed from oven. Allow to cool slightly before removing from pan. Slice and serve.

BETH'S CHICKEN DIJON

"Beth surprised us with this for dinner one night."

4 - 6 chicken breasts - skinned and boned	1 C chicken broth
3 Tbsp margarine	½ C half and half or evaporated milk
2 Tbsp flour	2 Tbsp Dijon mustard

Sauté chicken in butter over medium heat - about 10 minutes per side - and until golden brown. Remove to a warm platter. Blend flour into pan drippings. Stir until smooth and bubbly. Gradually stir in broth and then half and half. (See helpful hint # 10.) Cook until smooth and thickened. Stir in mustard. Return chicken to pan and simmer 10 minutes longer. Serves 4 - 6.

Beth Drummond

VEGETABLE CASSEROLE

1 can (16 oz) french cut beans - drained	½ C cheddar cheese - grated
1 can (16 oz) shoe peg corn - drained	1 can cream of celery soup
½ C chopped celery	1 jar pimento (2 oz) - chopped - optional
½ C chopped onion	salt and pepper to taste
½ C sour cream	

Mix all ingredients together. Place in a greased 1½ qt. casserole. Continued on opposite page.

VEGETABLE CASSEROLE TOPPING:

1 C cracker crumbs (Ritz)
½ stick melted butter
½ C slivered almonds

Mix ingredients and sprinkle over casserole. Bake at 350 degrees for 45 minutes. This makes a lot but freezes well. Serves 8.

BROILED TOMATOES

4 - 6 medium size tomatoes
Dijon mustard
2 - 3 slices bacon - cut in half

Cut stem end from tomatoes and set in greased muffin tin. Pour a little water in any unused muffin wells. Salt and pepper each tomato. Spread with Dijon mustard. Top with a piece of bacon. Bake at 350 degrees for 20 minutes. Run under the broiler to further brown bacon if needed.

REFRIGERATOR BREAD STICKS

Prepare refrigerator bread sticks as package directs. For a variation, dip sticks in melted butter and sprinkle with sesame seeds. Bake on aluminum foil lined bread pan.

LEMON ICE - BOX PIE

1 can sweetened condensed milk
1 tsp grated lemon rind
⅓ C lemon juice
8 oz frozen whipped topping - thawed
1 graham cracker crust - bought or made. (Mix 1 cup graham cracker crumbs with ½ cup melted butter. Press into pie plate. Chill while making filling.)

Mix condensed milk with lemon rind (See helpful hint # 13.) and lemon juice. Fold in whipped topping. Pour into crumb crust. Place in freezer at least one hour before serving.

BARBECUED CHICKEN

BEAN SALAD

JANE'S BATTER BREAD

&ᴸ FRESH STRAWBERRY PIE

BARBECUED CHICKEN

chicken pieces - everyone's favorite pieces
1 C tomato catsup
1 C Coke Classic
2 - 3 drops hot sauce

 Arrange chicken pieces in well greased baking dish. Mix equal parts of catsup and coke to make barbecue sauce. Add several drops of hot sauce. Salt and pepper chicken pieces. Pour sauce over chicken. Bake at 350 degrees for 1 hour. Turn or baste once during cooking time. May also cook on outdoor grill over medium hot coals.

Margaret E. Lee
DeLand, Florida

BEAN SALAD

1 can green beans
1 can wax beans
1 can kidney beans
1 can green beans and shellies
1 small purple onion - sliced thin
green pepper - chopped
½ C salad oil
½ C cider vinegar
1 C sugar

 Drain beans. Mix oil, vinegar and sugar until sugar dissolved. Pour over beans, onion and pepper. Refrigerate in container with tight fitting lid. Shake gently before serving. This salad will keep a week or more. Serves 8 - 10.

Betty Rose Sexton

JANE'S BATTER BREAD

"This is extra good."

1 C white corn meal
2 C boiling water
¾ tsp salt
4 Tbsp butter or margarine
4 eggs
1 C milk
2 Tbsp butter or margarine

Heat oven to 400 degrees. Put 2 Tbsp butter in a round casserole dish and melt in oven. Keep hot. Pour corn meal slowly into boiling water stirring constantly. Cook until mixture is thickened and smooth. Add 4 Tbsp butter and continue stirring until butter melts and mixture is "slick". This does not take very long. Beat eggs and mix with milk. Combine the two mixtures, blending well. Pour slowly into the hot casserole dish. Bake at 400 degrees for 30 - 45 minutes or until top is brown and center "set".

Jane Wootton

S P R I N G

FRESH STRAWBERRY PIE

1 9" crumb crust - bought or made (Mix 1 C graham
             cracker crumbs with ½ C melted
             butter. Press into pie plate.)
4 C fresh strawberries - sliced
1 C sugar
3 Tbsp cornstarch
2 Tbsp fresh lemon juice
dash salt
whipped topping

Mash 2 C strawberries. Mix with sugar, cornstarch and lemon juice. Cook over low heat until thickened. Place remaining 2 C berries in crumb crust. Pour cooked mixture over. Chill several hours. Serve with whipped topping.

MARGARET'S CHICKEN

RICE PILAF

TOSSED GREEN SALAD

ROSEMARY ROLLS

&. ANGEL FOOD CAKE DESERT

MARGARET'S CHICKEN

4 - 6 chicken breasts - boned and skinned
4 - 6 slices Swiss cheese
1 can cream chicken soup
½ can dry white wine
½ C slivered almonds

Place chicken breasts in greased baking dish. Cover each breast with a slice of Swiss cheese. Mix soup and wine. Spoon over chicken. Top with slivered almonds. Bake at 350 degrees for 1 hour.

Margaret B. Almond

RICE PILAF

Uncle Ben's Rice Pilaf with Rosemarina and Peas is delicious with this chicken dish.

Margaret B. Almond

TOSSED GREEN SALAD

Vary the combination of greens and vegetables. Alfalfa sprouts or bean sprouts make an interesting addition. Mix 1 - 2 Tbsp plain yogurt with Italian dressing to make a creamy Italian.

74

ROSEMARY ROLLS

1 pkg dry yeast
¾ C warm water (110 - 115 degrees)
2½ C biscuit mix
¼ C parmesan cheese
1¼ tsp crushed rosemary

Dissolve yeast in warm water. Mix in biscuit mix, cheese and rosemary. Beat with a fork until thoroughly blended. Turn dough onto floured surface. Knead just until smooth. Allow to rest 5 - 10 minutes. Form into a roll about 12" long. Cut into 12 pieces and shape into smooth balls. Place into greased muffin tins. Cover and allow to rise for about 30 minutes. Not absolutely necessary if time does not permit. Bake at 400 degrees for 15 - 20 minutes. Makes 1 dozen.

ANGEL FOOD CAKE DESSERT

1 angel food cake loaf
1 can cherry pie filling
1 large container Cool Whip

Slice off top of cake loaf. Scoop out center and fill with pie filling. Replace top. Ice the entire cake with Cool Whip. Refrigerate until serving time. Slice to serve.

Nettie M. Sutphin
Camden, South Carolina

75

FIRST WARM DAY PICNIC

FRIED CHICKEN

POTATO SALAD

CRUDITE

FRENCH BREAD

FRESH FRUIT and CHEESE

"The first warm day in spring makes us all want to be outside. Have an impromptu picnic. Don't try to plan it, just do it when that special day comes."

FRIED CHICKEN

Buy your favorite.

POTATO SALAD

Buy your favorite.

CRUDITE

broccoli - cut into bite size pieces
carrot sticks
celery sticks
cherry tomatoes
1 C mayonnaise
2 Tbsp salad mustard

Arrange fresh vegetables in a basket lined with a brightly colored napkin. Mix mayonnaise and mustard. Put it in a bowl in the center of the basket. Decorate with fresh parsley and a blossom or two from the yard.

FRENCH BREAD

Buy bread. Serve with softened butter. Place it on a napkin and pull pieces off.

FRESH FRUIT AND CHEESE

Arrange a tray of apples, grapes, and cheese.

Make this a real picnic. Use paper plates and plastic forks and eat outside. The family will enjoy the celebration. Let it be an annual occasion!

NOTES for FUTURE PICNICS

SPRING

BREADED SOFT - SHELL CRABS

COTTAGE FRIES

COLE SLAW

CORN BREAD

STRAWBERRY TRIFLE

BREADED SOFT - SHELL CRABS

soft - shell crabs - purchase at fish market. Allow at
  lease 3 per adult.
1 egg beaten
1 C milk
¾ C corn meal
¼ C flour
dash of salt
oil for frying
1 lemon
tartar sauce

Mix egg and milk. Mix meal, flour and salt. First dip crabs in
milk mixture then in meal. Set on waxed paper until all are ready.
In a heavy skillet or electric frying pan add oil up to 1 inch deep.
Heat moderately high. Add crabs so as not to crowd. Fry until
golden on each side. It doesn't take long so watch closely. Remove
to paper towels to drain then to oven proof platter to keep warm.
Serve with tartar sauce and lemon wedges. This recipe is also
good for fried oysters.

COTTAGE FRIES

large baking potatoes
margarine

Scrub potatoes. Cut in thick wedges leaving skin on. Rub with
softened margarine. Set up (skin down) on a foil lined pan.
Sprinkle with salt. Place in 350 degree oven for 40 - 45 minutes.

COLE SLAW

1 medium head cabbage - shredded
2 - 3 carrots - grated
2 - 3 green onions with tops - chopped
Marzetti Slaw Dressing

Lightly toss prepared vegetables. Stir in enough Marzetti dressing to hold together. Refrigerate.

Margaret B. Almond

CORN BREAD

1 C self-rising flour
1 C self-rising cornmeal
½ tsp salt
2 Tbsp oil

1 egg
½ tsp sugar
1 C milk

Mix flour, meal and salt. Make a well in dry ingredients and pour in oil and egg. Stir with a fork. Add sugar and milk. Stir until smooth. Pour into a hot greased iron skillet or baking dish. Bake at 400 degrees for 20 - 25 minutes. Outside should be very brown.

STRAWBERRY TRIFLE

1 small package instant vanilla pudding mix
1¾ C milk
1 4 oz container frozen whipped topping - thawed
sponge cake or pound cake
⅓ C fresh orange juice
2 C strawberries - sliced
2 - 3 Tbsp powdered sugar
slivered almonds

Sprinkle sliced strawberries with 2 - 3 Tbsp powdered sugar. Set aside. Combine pudding mix and milk. Stir until smooth. Refrigerate. Cut cake into 1 inch cubes. Place in bottom of a trifle bowl or any glass serving bowl. Sprinkle with orange juice. Spoon strawberries evenly over cake cubes. Spread pudding mix over berries. Cover with whipped topping. Sprinkle with slivered almonds. Refrigerate until serving time.

CRABMEAT CASSEROLE

"This is the only dish I ever fixed which I didn't insist the children take three bites. It was too good to "waste" that way. As you might guess, they all enjoy it now."

1 lb backfin crabmeat
3 Tbsp butter or margarine
3 Tbsp flour
1 C milk
salt and white pepper
2 - 3 Tbsp sherry (optional)
1 C grated sharp cheese
1 C bread crumbs
¼ C butter or margarine - melted

Pick over crabmeat and remove any shell. Melt butter in heavy sauce pan, add flour and blend until smooth. Add milk and stir constantly until smooth and thickened. (Heat milk in microwave before adding to speed up this step.) Season to taste and stir in sherry if desired. Combine with crabmeat. Place in a sprayed casserole. Top with buttered bread crumbs (See helpful hint # 9.) and grated cheese. Heat in a 350 degree over for 15 - 20 minutes or until it is bubbly hot and cheese has melted. Recipe may be doubled.

1969 - Mother, Elizabeth F. Easley

FRESH ASPARAGUS SPEARS - Select about a pound of asparagus. Trim tough ends. Cut into thin strips - this is especially good for the larger spears. In a skillet with a top, melt 3 Tbsp butter. Add the asparagus. Cover and simmer 3 - 5 minutes. Gently remove to a serving platter. Drizzle butter and juice of half a lemon over. Salt to taste. Serves 4.

CRESCENT ROLL-UPS

1 pkg refrigerator crescent rolls
4 - 5 slices very thin cured ham
soft butter

Spread each crescent roll with soft butter and add a small strip of ham. Roll up in usual way. Cook as package directs.

STRAWBERRY SHORTCAKE

1 yellow cake mix
1 large carton frozen whipped topping - thawed
1 qt fresh strawberries

Make cake as package directs. Cool layers completely. Split layers in half, making four. (See helpful hint # 23.) Spread each layer with whipped topping and cover with sliced strawberries. Frost entire cake with topping. Add whole berries for garnish. Refrigerate. This is a big pretty cake to serve at the table.

SPRING

SHAD ROE

shad roe sets - amount needed
6 - 8 slices bacon
lemon juice
lemon wedges
salt and pepper to taste

Fry bacon in heavy skillet or electric fry pan. Remove and drain. Wrap each set of roe in waxed paper - envelope style. Secure with wooden tooth picks. Fry roe in bacon drippings over medium high heat turning several times. Cut away paper and transfer to serving platter. Sprinkle with lemon juice and season. Serve with lemon wedges.

Jane P. Wootton

CORN SPOONBREAD

1 pkg (8½ oz) cornbread mix
1 can (8 oz) cream style corn
1 can (8 oz) whole kernel corn - drained
2 eggs - slightly beaten
1 C sour cream
¼ C margarine - melted

Beat eggs. Add cornbread mix. Stir in the remaining ingredients. Pour into a greased baking dish. Bake at 350 degrees for 45 minutes. Serves 6 - 8.

Marguerite Crumbley

24 - HOUR SLAW

1 large cabbage - shredded
1 purple onion - thinly sliced
1 - 2 carrots grated
1 C sugar - divided
1 tsp celery seeds
1 tsp dry mustard
1½ tsp salt
1 C cider vinegar
1 C oil

Prepare vegetables. Add ¾ cup sugar and gently toss. Bring ¼ cup sugar and remaining ingredients except oil to a boil. Add oil and bring back to boil. Pour hot dressing over vegetable mixture. Do not stir. Cover and immediately refrigerate. Chill 24 hours. Stir before serving. Keeps well in the refrigerator.

CAROLYN'S COOKIES - POUND CAKE WAFERS

2½ sticks real butter
1 C sugar
2 egg yolks
3 C sifted flour
1 tsp vanilla
pecan halves

Cream butter. Add sugar gradually. Add egg yolks one at a time. Add flour gradually. Add vanilla last. Drop by teaspoon on ungreased cookie sheet. Press pecan half on top before baking. Bake at 350 degrees for 12 - 15 minutes. Makes about 75.

Mrs. Robert Griffith Jones - Carolyn
Virginia Beach, Virginia

PINEAPPLE SHERBET - Serve sherbet garnished with a sprig of mint or strawberry. A teaspoon of créme de menthe is nice for adults.

CRAB CAKES

STUFFED TOMATOES

SPINACH AND CHEESE

GRIDDLE CAKES

❧ POUND CAKE

CRAB CAKES

1 lb backfin crabmeat	2 tsp Worcestershire sauce
2 eggs - beaten	3 - 4 generous shakes of
3 Tbsp mayonnaise	hot sauce
2 tsp dry mustard	½ C fine cracker crumbs

Pick over crabmeat and discard any shell. Stir together all other ingredients then add crabmeat. Flatten into cakes. Fry on hot skillet which has been sprayed with a non-stick spray until lightly brown. May transfer to an oven proof platter, cover with aluminum foil and keep warm in a moderate oven. Serve with tartar sauce and lemon wedges. Serves 4.

Margarett Pendleton

STUFFED TOMATOES

4 medium tomatoes	¼ C chicken stock
1½ - 2 C cooked rice	1 Tbsp chopped basil -
1 Tbsp margarine - melted	fresh
1 Tbsp chopped green onion	salt and pepper to taste

Cut stem end tops from tomatoes. Scoop out centers with a spoon. Sprinkle with salt and invert on paper towels. Mix rice (See helpful hint # 3.) and other ingredients. Salt and pepper to taste. Spoon rice mixture into tomato cups. Place in muffin tins. (See helpful hint # 35.) Heat at 350 degrees for about 5 - 10 minutes. Serves 4.

SPINACH AND CHEESE

1 lb fresh spinach
6 slices bacon - cooked and
  crumbled
1 can sliced water chest-
  nuts - drained

1 jar (16 oz) Cheese Whiz
1 Tbsp margarine

Wash fresh spinach three times to remove all grit. Remove tough stems. Steam spinach in a vegetable steamer until just wilted. Drain. Melt 1 Tbsp margarine in a greased 8" baking dish. Place spinach in bottom. Sprinkle bacon and water chestnuts on top. Melt Cheese Whiz in microwave and spoon over. Place in a 350 degree oven until just heated. About 5 - 10 minutes.

GRIDDLE CAKES

½ C self-rising corn meal
1 - 1¼ C buttermilk

1 egg - beaten
1 Tbsp butter - melted

Mix all ingredients with a fork. Have batter thin. Add more milk if necessary. (See helpful hint #15.) Spoon onto hot greased griddle. Makes small light cakes. Serve with lots of butter.

POUND CAKE

"This cake is good plain or with ice cream and fruit or chocolate sauce."

1 stick butter
½ C solid shortening
3 C sugar
6 eggs
3 C flour

1 tsp salt
1 tsp baking powder
1 C milk
1 tsp vanilla
1 tsp lemon extract

Cream butter, shortening and sugar. Add eggs one at a time. Sift dry ingredients together. Add to creamed mixture alternately with milk, beginning and ending with flour. Add flavorings. Pour into a greased and floured tube pan. Place in a COLD oven. Turn temperature to 350 degrees and bake 1 hour.

Etta Mae Neal
Danville, Virginia

LONDON BROIL

1 **London Broil**

MARINADE:

¼ C water
¼ C soy sauce
¼ C **honey**

garlic salt
½ tsp ginger

Pierce London Broil with a fork. Sprinkle each side with garlic salt and ¼ tsp ginger. Rub into meat. Mix marinade and pour over meat. (See helpful hint # 22.) Marinate overnight. Broil meat about 7 - 8 minutes per side for medium. Slice very thin. Heat remaining marinade and pour over meat.

GREAT POTATO CASSEROLE

2 lb bag **frozen hash brown potatoes**
1 tsp salt
¼ tsp pepper
½ C chopped green onions
1 can **cream of chicken soup** - undiluted

1 pt (16 oz) **sour cream**
2 C grated sharp cheese
½ stick butter
½ C crushed **cornflakes**

Mix all ingredients except butter and cornflakes. Place in a greased oblong baking dish. Cut up butter on top and sprinkle crushed cornflakes over. Bake at 350 degrees for 45 minutes. Serves 6.

Margaret Easley Lee
Deland, Florida

TOSSED GREEN SALAD

Use a mixture of greens: spinach, endive, iceberg lettuce, fresh snipped parsley, chives, and sweet basil. Add chopped celery and carrots, sliced fresh mushrooms and cocktail tomatoes. A few sunflower seeds sprinkled over adds a different flavor. Toss with your favorite dressing.

LOAF BREAD - Serve a crusty loaf of bakery bread at room temperature with soft butter.

ECLAIRS

"This is easy and fun!"

PASTRY:

1 stick <u>butter</u> - no substitute

1 C water

1 C flour

4 eggs

Bring butter and water to boil. Remove from heat and stir in flour until smooth. Add eggs one at a time and mix until glossy. Use a portable hand mixer. Drop by teaspoonfuls onto a greased baking sheet. Bake at 350 degrees for 30 minutes. Slit the tops then bake 10 minutes longer. Leftover pastries are great filled with chicken or seafood salad. Makes about 15.

FILLING:

1 package <u>instant vanilla pudding mix</u>

½ C frozen <u>whipped topping</u> - thawed

1½ C cold milk

Make pudding with milk. Fold in whipped topping. Refrigerate to set. Spoon filling into "cavity" of pastry.

CHOCOLATE SAUCE:

1 <u>square unsweetened chocolate</u>

½ C sugar

1 Tbsp butter

pinch salt

1 small can (5 oz) <u>evaporated milk</u>

Heat in heavy sauce pan, stirring constantly. Spoon over filled eclairs.

Mary Collins

SAUTÉED VEAL and FRESH MUSHROOMS

FETTUCCINI

VEGETABLE MEDLEY

HERB CHEESE BREAD

❧ ICE CREAM PIE

SAUTÉED VEAL and FRESH MUSHROOMS

½ lb **veal - thinly sliced**
flour for dredging
1 - 1½ C sliced **fresh mushrooms**
4 Tbsp butter or margarine
1 C **chicken broth**

1 **lemon**
3 Tbsp cold butter or margarine
fresh **parsley**
salt and pepper to taste

Dredge veal slices in flour and sauté in butter. Cook about 2 minutes per side. Do not crowd pieces. Remove and set aside. Sauté the fresh mushrooms. Set aside. Add chicken broth and juice of half the lemon. Replace cooked veal and mushrooms. Cook for another 2 minutes. Remove with a slotted spoon to serving platter. Turn heat in pan to high and reduce pan juices by half. Cut in 3 Tbsp butter, salt, pepper and about a tablespoon of minced parsley. Cook only until butter melts. Spoon sauce over veal and mushrooms. Garnish with remaining half lemon cut in thin slices and fresh parsley sprigs. Serves 4.

FETTUCCINI

½ - 1 lb **fettuccini**
3 - 4 Tbsp butter - melted
½ C parmesan cheese

salt
parsley flakes - fresh or
dried

Cook fettuccini in large pot of lightly salted water. Boil 10 - 12 minutes or until tender. Drain. Replace in pot and toss with 3 Tbsp melted butter (add more if needed). Stir in cheese, salt and parsley. (Basil may be substituted for parsley.) Serves 4 - 6.

VEGETABLE MEDLEY

1 whole cucumber - thinly sliced
4 - 6 cocktail tomatoes - halved
3 large fresh mushrooms - sliced
2 green onions with tops - chopped
1 - 2 stalks of celery - slice diagonally
2 carrots - slice on diagonal
oil and vinegar salad dressing

Arrange chilled vegetables in a salad bowl. Pour an oil and vinegar salad dressing over it and replace in refrigerator until serving time. Serves 4.

HERB CHEESE BREAD

2 C Bisquick
1 tsp sugar
2 tsp dried onion flakes
1 egg
½ C milk

¼ C melted butter
¼ C dry white wine
⅓ C grated parmesan
   cheese - divided
½ tsp dried oregano

Combine dry ingredients in a bowl. Beat egg with milk. Add to dry mixture. Add butter, wine and all but 2 Tbsp cheese. Mix well. Pour into greased round casserole. Sprinkle reserved cheese on top. Bake at 400 degrees for 25 minutes. Cut in wedges to serve.

ICE CREAM PIE

1 (6 oz) package semi-sweet chocolate chips
1 stick butter
1 Tbsp water
4 C Special K cereal
2 qts peppermint ice cream
grated chocolate or chocolate sauce for garnish

In heavy sauce pan over low heat melt the chocolate chips with butter and water. Add cereal and mix thoroughly. Divide mixture into two 9" pie pans and pack for crust. Place in freezer until completely frozen. Add 1 quart of softened ice cream into each pie crust. (One may be saved for another time.) Keep in freezer until ready to serve. May garnish with grated chocolate or drizzle a little chocolate sauce over.

MARINATED FLANK STEAK

1½ - 2 lb flank steak
1 - 2 lemons
onion salt
fresh ground pepper

Open steak out flat and score both sides diagonally with a sharp knife. Sprinkle both sides generously with onion salt and pepper and rub into meat. Place in shallow pan for marinating. Squeeze ½ lemon over each side. Use more if lemons are not very juicy. Marinate at least 3 hours; turn once. (See helpful hint # 22.) Broil steak 5 minutes per side. Serve thinly sliced. Heat marinade and pour over meat. Serves 4 - 5.

BAKED POTATOES - Wash and grease potatoes with bacon drippings or margarine. Prick skin with a fork. Bake at 350 degrees for 1 hour or until soft to touch. Serve split with lots of butter. Sour cream with chives and grated sharp cheese may be added.

BEER MUFFINS

1 C biscuit mix
1 Tbsp sugar
4 oz beer

Stir ingredients together with a fork until smooth. Dark beer makes lovely brown muffins. Spoon into greased muffin tins. Bake at 400 degrees for 20 minutes. Makes 6.

GREEN PEA CASSEROLE

1 stick margarine
1 green pepper - diced
1 medium onion - chopped
1 C chopped celery
1 can mushroom soup
1 can sliced water chestnuts - drained
2 cans green peas (LeSueur) - drained
1 small jar pimento - drained - optional

Sauté pepper, onion and celery in margarine until just tender. Add undiluted soup, water chestnuts and pimento. Simmer until heated. In a greased casserole add 1 can of peas, half of the soup and vegetable mixture, the other can of peas and top with remaining mixture. Bake at 350 degrees for about 20 minutes. This makes a lot. It may be divided into 2 smaller casseroles and frozen. Serves 6 - 8.

COCONUT POUND CAKE

"This is a big cake. Keeps well and freezes well."

¾ lb butter
3 C sugar
6 eggs
3 C flour
1 C sour cream

¼ tsp salt
¼ tsp soda
1 tsp vanilla
6 - 7 oz grated coconut

Have all ingredients at room temperature. Cream butter and sugar. Add eggs one at a time and beat well after each. Add flour, salt, soda, sour cream, and vanilla. Beat well. Add coconut last and blend evenly. Pour into a greased and floured tube pan. Bake at 350 degrees for 1 hour and 15 minutes. Cool cake on rack in the pan. (See helpful hint # 8.)

SALMON LOAF

1 lb can salmon
⅓ C celery - chopped
⅓ C green pepper
⅓ C minced green onion
½ C fine bread crumbs
½ C mayonnaise
2 eggs - beaten
½ lemon - juiced
salt to taste

Drain salmon, flake, and remove bone and skin. Combine all ingredients and pack into a small greased loaf pan. Bake 45 minutes at 350 degrees. Serves 4 - 6.

1984 - Staige D. Nolley

SAUCE:

¼ C mayonnaise
½ C sour cream
1 tsp Dijon mustard
1 Tbsp horseradish
1 - 2 green onions with tops - minced

Stir all ingredients together and refrigerate until serving time. Serve in a bowl accompanying salmon loaf.

NEW RED POTATOES - Select small red potatoes. Wash but do not peel. Boil in lightly salted water until tender. Drain. Add butter and snipped fresh parsley.

FRESH SPINACH SALAD

1 lb <u>fresh spinach</u> - washed and stemmed
<u>bean sprouts</u> - canned or fresh
6 - 8 slices <u>bacon</u> - cooked and crumbled
3 hard cooked eggs - chopped
1 <u>purple onion</u> - thinly sliced

Layer in a large salad bowl.

DRESSING:

1 C salad oil
½ C sugar
⅓ C catsup

¼ C vinegar
1 medium onion - grated

Mix in a jar and shake vigorously. Pour over salad.

LIGHT MUFFINS

2 C self-rising flour
1 C sweet milk
4 Tbsp <u>herb salad dressing</u> or homemade mayonnaise

Mix ingredients. For herb salad dressing: Blend 1 envelope Creamy Herb Ranch Salad Dressing Mix, 1 C mayonnaise, and 1 C plain yogurt. Spoon batter into greased muffin tins. Bake at 350 degrees for 15 minutes. Makes 12.

NO-CRUST COCONUT PIE

4 eggs
1¾ C sugar
½ C self-rising flour
1 can (7 oz) <u>grated coconut</u>

2 C milk
1 tsp vanilla
¼ C butter - melted
dash salt

Beat eggs. Combine sugar and flour then stir into eggs. Add remaining ingredients. Pour into a greased 10 inch pie plate. Bake at 350 degrees for 40 - 45 minutes or until set. This makes a large pie.

BARBECUED SPARERIBS

spareribs - country style or back ribs

SAUCE:
1 C cider vinegar
2 Tbsp sugar
2 Tbsp Worcestershire
½ C catsup
1 tsp dry mustard
1 tsp paprika
salt and pepper

Place ribs in sprayed shallow baking dish. Combine sauce ingredients and simmer for 15 minutes. Pour barbecue sauce over ribs and bake at 350 degrees for 1 hour. May be cooked on a charcoal grill over medium hot coals for about 45 minutes. Baste and turn frequently.

Mother, Elizabeth F. Easley

POTATO BAKE

4 thawed squares of Ore Ida Hash Browns
2 C cheddar cheese - grated
1 pt sour cream
2 cans cream of potato soup - undiluted

Mix cheese and sour cream with undiluted soup. Break up hash brown squares and stir into cheese mixture. Pour into greased casserole. Bake at 350 degrees for 1 hour. Serves 6.

Margie Ayres

TOSSED SALAD - As fresh vegtables come into season, add them to the salad for variety: thinly sliced small yellow squash, cucumbers and radishes.

LACY GRIDDLE CAKES

¾ C cornmeal
1 C milk
1 egg
½ tsp salt
2 Tbsp melted margarine

Beat the egg until light. Add milk. Slowly add cornmeal and salt. Mix well and add melted margarine. Drop by tablespoonfuls on hot greased griddle. Flip to brown on both sides. Stir batter each time.

CHOCOLATE SUNDAE

vanilla ice cream
maraschino cherry
whipped topping
chopped nuts - optional

CHOCOLATE SAUCE

½ C evaporated milk
1 Tbsp butter
4 envelopes of instant hot chocolate mix with mini-
   marshallows

Heat milk and butter. Add envelopes of chocolate. Stirring constantly, cook for 1 - 2 minutes until slightly thickened. Serve hot over ice cream. Top with nuts, whipped topping and a cherry. Keep any remaining sauce in refrigerator. Reheat in microwave as needed. Makes about 1 cup.

SWEET and SOUR PORK

RICE

SNOW PEA PODS

RICE CAKES

ᢶ LADYFINGER LAYER CAKE

SWEET and SOUR PORK

1½ - 2 lbs <u>boneless pork shoulder or loin</u>
2 Tbsp cooking oil
1 can (20 oz) <u>pineapple chunks</u>
¾ C water
¼ C vinegar
1 Tbsp soy sauce
¼ C brown sugar - firmly packed
½ tsp salt
2 Tbsp cornstarch
2 Tbsp water
⅓ C onion - thinly sliced
1 <u>green pepper</u> - thin strips

Cut pork into short strips about ½ inch thick. Sauté in oil until lightly browned. Drain meat and place in a Dutch oven or casserole with a tight fitting lid. Drain juice from pineapple chunks and combine with ¾ C water, vinegar, soy sauce, brown sugar, and salt. Pour over meat and place in a 350 degree oven for 1 hour. Check meat during cooking time and add a little more water if needed. Remove from the oven. Dissolve cornstarch in 2 Tbsp water and stir into meat. Add pineapple chunks, onions and pepper. Cover and return to oven for about 15 minutes longer. Serve over a mound of fluffy white rice. Serves 6.

RICE - Prepare enough rice to yield 2 - 3 cups of cooked rice.

SNOW PEA PODS - fresh or frozen. Wash and trim if fresh. Sauté in butter or margarine until thoroughly heated but still retains the bright green color. Salt to taste.

RICE CAKES - Purchase at the market. An interesting accompaniment.

LADYFINGER LAYER CAKE

1 C butter or margarine - softened
2 C powdered sugar
4 eggs
1 can (13¼ oz) crushed pineapple - drained
1 C chopped pecans
2 doz. ladyfingers - split
½ pt whipped cream or frozen whipped topping

Cream butter and sugar until light and fluffy. Beat in eggs one at a time. Add pineapple and nuts. Mix well. Line a loaf pan with waxed paper. Pack the bottom of the pan with split ladyfingers - fill in the "holes" with broken pieces. Make a layer of the pineapple filling. Continue until pan is full. Cover and refrigerate 6 - 8 hours or overnight. Unmold on cake plate and ice with whipped cream or thawed topping. Garnish with mint leaves and additional chopped pecans. Serves 8.

NOTES

F.E.D.

S U M M E R

SUMMER

MAIN DISHES

Shish-K-Bob • Marinated Chuck Roast • Stuffed Zucchini • Cream of Asparagus Soup • Shrimp Remoulade • Grilled Chicken • Polynesian Chicken Salad • Barbecued Chicken • Delux Turkey Sandwiches • Gazpacho • Swiss Omelet Roll • Grilled Ham Steak • Sea Leg Salad • Summer Salad • Fettuccini with Crab • Hearty Parmigiana • Chicken with Sauce • Tarragon Chicken Salad • Flounder Fillets • London Broil with Burgundy Sauce • Teriyaki Flank Steak

VEGETABLES

Rice • Green Beans • Corn on the Cob • Buttered Noodles • Zucchini Casserole • Marinated Vegetables • Baked Beans • Zucchini Bake • Fresh Asparagus • Sliced Tomatoes • Green and Gold Casserole • Butter Beans • Baked Tomato • Squash Casserole • Mustard Potatoes

SALADS

Spinach • Sliced Cucumbers • Green Pea • Cole Slaw • Lettuce and Tomatoes • Quick and Easy Tomato Aspic • Crisp Slaw • Tomato and Cuke • Lime-Grape Gelatin Mold • Layered • Tossed Green

BREADS

Bakery Loaf with Herbed Butter • Herb Bread • Garlic Bread • Sesame Bread Sticks • Lemon Muffins • Pull Apart Loaf • Corn Muffins • Cheese Bread • Cheese and Herb Bread • Spoon Cornbread • Mayo Muffins • Ham Biscuits • Buttermilk Muffins

DESSERTS

Watermelon • Peach Cobbler • Fresh Pineapple with Lemon Topping • Lime Ice-Box Pie • Canteloupe Rings • Banana Split Cake • Blender Chocolate Pie • German Chocolate Pie • Lemon Ice-Box Cake • Old Fashioned Peach Ice Cream • Ice Cream Cake • Orange Chiffon Cake • Lemon Bisque • Sherbet Cake • Peppermint Brownies • Fresh Fruit Torte • Macaroon Ice Cream Dessert • Fudge Sundae Pie • Libbie's Fruit Cobbler • Blackberry Cobbler

SHISH-K-BOB

RICE CASSEROLE

SPINACH SALAD

BAKERY LOAF with HERBED BUTTER

WATERMELON

SHISH-K-BOB

beef - sirloin or round steak
green pepper - cut in wide strips
onion - quartered and separated
mushroom caps
cherry tomatoes
1 pkg Adolph's marinade for steak

Cut beef in chunks - not too large so that meat will cook before vegetables over-cook. Allow 6 - 8 chunks per adult. Prepare Adolph's marinade as package directs and marinate meat for about 30 minutes. This adds flavor as well as tenderizing. Alternate meat and vegetables on skewer. Cook over medium hot coals on out-door grill. Serve over rice.

RICE CASSEROLE

1 C Uncle Ben's regular rice
1 can beef bouillon
1 soup can plus ½ cup water
chopped celery
1 stick margarine
paprika

In a greased oblong baking dish spread rice then add liquids. Add celery. Dot with margarine. Sprinkle generously with paprika. Bake at 350 degrees for 1 hour. Serves 4 - 6.

SPINACH SALAD

fresh spinach - about a pound
bean sprouts - canned and drained - or fresh
6 strips bacon - cooked and crumbled
3 hard cooked eggs
1 purple onion or 3 - 4 green onions

DRESSING:

1 C salad oil
½ C sugar
¼ C vinegar
⅓ C catsup
1 medium onion - grated
dash salt

Mix dressing in a jar with a tight fitting lid. Shake well and refrigerate. It keeps indefinitely. Wash spinach. Tear off stems and tear into bite-size pieces. Chop 2 eggs (See helpful hint # 19.) and slice one to garnish top of salad. Slice onion into rings. Mix all ingredients and toss with dressing.

BAKERY LOAF

Split loaf length wise.

HERBED BUTTER:

1 stick butter - softened
1 Tbsp fresh basil or chives (1 tsp dried)
¼ tsp onion salt

Spread on bread. Toast under broiler or put halves back together, wrap in foil and heat in oven.

WATERMELON

Serve watermelon well chilled. Let children take slices outside to eat!

MARINATED CHUCK ROAST

GREEN BEANS - SLICED TOMATOES

CORN ON COB

HERB BREAD

PEACH COBBLER

MARINATED CHUCK ROAST - GRILLED

3 - 5 lb chuck roast
meat tenderizer

MARINADE:

3 Tbsp margarine
1 Tbsp sesame seeds
½ C strong coffee
½ C soy sauce

1 Tbsp Worcestershire
sauce
1 Tbsp vinegar
1 medium onion - grated

Prick roast deeply with fork and rub each side with tenderizer. In a sauce pan put sesame seeds and margarine. When margarine has melted add remaining ingredients and bring to boil. Pour immediately over roast. Cover and refrigerate over night. Remove from the refrigerator at least an hour before cooking. (See helpful hint # 11.) Have charcoal fire moderately hot. Cook roast 30 - 45 minutes per side - depending on thickness. Keep grill top closed except to baste and turn every 15 minutes until desired doneness. Heat remaining marinade and serve with meat.

GREEN BEANS

1 - 1½ lbs tender young green beans
Italian Salad dressing

Wash and trim green beans. Drop into boiling water for 3 - 5 minutes. Remove and plunge immediately into ice water. Drain. Pour salad dressing over and marinate in the refrigerator until serving time. (See helpful hint # 22.) Serves 4 - 6.

TOMATOES - Sliced summer tomatoes are a delicious addition to any meal.

CORN ON COB - Select tender well filled out <u>ears of corn.</u> Shuck and trim ends. Cover corn with cold water and bring to a boil. Allow to boil briskly for 3 - 5 minutes. Drain and serve with lots of butter.

HERB BREAD

2 C <u>biscuit mix</u>
1 Tbsp sugar
2 tsp dried onion flakes
½ tsp oregano
1 egg - beaten
½ C milk
¼ C margarine - melted
¼ C <u>dry white wine</u>
⅓ C parmesan cheese

Combine dry ingredients. Stir in liquids and beaten egg. Add all except 2 Tbsp of the parmesan cheese. Pour into a greased round casserole. Sprinkle reserved cheese on top. Bake at 400 degrees for 25 minutes. Transfer to a serving plate and cut in wedges.

PEACH COBBLER

<u>pie crust</u> for a 2 crust deep dish pie
8 - 10 well-ripened <u>peaches</u>
1¼ - 1½ C sugar
1 - 2 Tbsp flour
4 - 6 Tbsp margarine
nutmeg
salt

Roll bottom pie crust large enough to fall well over edges of a square or oblong Pyrex baking dish. Peel and slice peaches allowing all juice to fall into bowl. Sprinkle with sugar - amount depends on ripeness and sweetness of peaches. Sprinkle with flour and stir. Add a generous dusting of nutmeg (See helpful hint # 7.) and a dash of salt. Pour peaches into crust and dot with margarine. Roll top crust to cover. Fold and pinch edges to seal. Prick top with a fork. Pre-heat oven to 500 degrees. Put pie in oven and turn immediately to 350 degrees. Bake about 1 hour. *"Nutmeg is the secret."*

My Aunt, Margaret F. Hankins

STUFFED ZUCCHINI

2 lbs medium size zucchini
½ lb ground beef
¼ C mayonnaise
2 - 3 green onions
2 Tbsp fresh parsley flakes
  (2 tsp dried)

1 tsp dried oregano
⅔ - 1 C spaghetti sauce
  with mushrooms
1 Tbsp lemon juice
⅓ C parmesan cheese
salt and pepper to taste

Brown beef just until red is gone. (See helpful hint # 2.) Drain thoroughly. Split zucchini lengthwise. Discard seeds. Scoop out center pulp leaving about ¼ inch shell. Pat dry. Chop zucchini pulp. Add to beef and remaining ingredients. Fill zucchini shells with beef mixture. Place in greased shallow baking dish. Bake at 350 degrees for 45 minutes. Top with additional parmesan cheese. Serves 4 - 6.

BUTTERED NOODLES

1 pkg flat noodles
3 Tbsp butter or margarine
4 Tbsp fresh herbs from garden
    (chives, parsley, basil or dill)
¼ C parmesan cheese

Cook noodles as package directs. Rinse and drain. Top with butter, fresh herbs (See helpful hint # 26.) and parmesan cheese. Place in greased casserole dish and keep warm in oven until serving time. Serves 6.

SLICED CUCUMBERS

3 - 4 cucumbers

Peel and thinly slice cucumbers. Cover with a few ice cubes and keep in refrigerator until almost serving time. This makes them really crisp. Drain and pat with paper towels. Season with salt and pepper and parsley for color. Toss with your choice of dressing. This makes a refreshing summer salad.

GARLIC BREAD

Slice a large bakery loaf of bread lengthwise. Spread with soft butter then sprinkle with garlic salt.

FRESH PINEAPPLE with LEMON TOPPING

fresh pineapple - peeled, cored and sliced
1 pkg instant lemon pudding mix
1 C milk
2 C frozen whipped topping - thawed
berries and mint for garnish

Mix milk with instant pudding mix. Fold in thawed topping. Top each slice of fresh pineapple with lemon pudding mixture. Garnish with fresh strawberries or blueberries and a sprig of mint.

NOTES

SUMMER

107

CREAM of ASPARAGUS SOUP

SHRIMP REMOULADE

SESAME BREAD STICKS

❧ LIME ICE-BOX PIE

CREAM of ASPARAGUS SOUP

3 C chopped asparagus spears
1 tsp salt
½ tsp garlic salt
¼ tsp white pepper
1½ C medium white sauce: 3 Tbsp butter, 3 Tbsp flour,
       1½ C half and half or evaporated milk.

Cover asparagus with salted water and simmer until very tender - about 40 minutes. Meanwhile make a white sauce by melting butter in a heavy sauce pan. Blend in flour and allow to bubble a few seconds. Add milk and stir until thickened. Puree asparagus in blender and force through a strainer or sieve. Should be about 2 C. Discard pulp. Add puree to white sauce. Add seasonings. Serve hot or cold. Garnish with a dollop of sour cream and chopped chives. (If I get to make this ahead, I serve it cold. If not, I have it hot. It's good either way.)

SHRIMP REMOULADE

1 lb fresh or frozen shrimp
2 eggs - hard cooked
1 avocado
lettuce

Shred lettuce. Mound shrimp on top. Garnish with hard cooked egg and avocado. Top with remoulade sauce.

REMOULADE SAUCE:

1 C mayonnaise - Hellmann's
⅓ C bottled chili sauce
2 Tbsp hot and spicy mustard
1 Tbsp horseradish (more if desired)
2 shakes hot sauce
1 green onion with top - chopped fine
2 ribs celery - chopped fine
¼ C sweet pickle relish - drained

Mix all sauce ingredients together. Refrigerate until serving time.

SESAME BREAD STICKS

1 pkg refrigerator bread sticks
butter or margarine
sesame seeds

Dip each bread strip in butter before twisting. Sprinkle with sesame seeds. Bake on a foil lined pan as package directs.

LIME ICE-BOX PIE

1 crumb crust (bought or made)
1 (3 oz) box lime gelatin
1 (8 oz) carton frozen whipped topping - thawed

Make crumb crust by mixing 1 C graham cracker crumbs with ½ stick melted butter. Press into pie pan. Mix gelatin with 1 C boiling water. Stir to dissolve. Chill to egg white consistency. If it gets too firm, beat with mixer. Fold in whipped topping. Spoon into pie crust. Garnish with a mint sprig. Refrigerate until serving time - about 1 hour.

GRILLED CHICKEN

chicken pieces - as needed
1 stick margarine
1 lemon - juiced
2 Tbsp Worcestershire
seasoned salt
fresh ground pepper

Prepare charcoal grill and medium hot fire. (See helpful hint # 37.) Remove skin from chicken pieces. Melt margarine. Add lemon juice and Worcestershire sauce. Place chicken on grill and baste frequently. Sprinkle each side with salt and pepper. Turn several times. It will need to cook 45 minutes to 1 hour depending on how hot the coals are. Remove to serving platter. Pour any remaining basting mixture over. May bake in oven at 350 degrees for 1 hour.

CORN on COB - Select tender well filled out <u>ears of corn</u>. Shuck and trim ends. Put in a large pot and cover with water. Place cold on the stove and bring to boil. Allow to boil 3 - 5 minutes. Remove to a serving platter and butter generously.

ZUCCHINI CASSEROLE

2 medium zucchini
2 - 3 tomatoes
2 - 3 green onions
3 - 4 Tbsp margarine
Velveta cheese
salt and pepper

Melt butter and put a little in bottom of a greased baking dish. Make a single layer of thinly sliced zucchini, then sliced tomatoes and a sprinkling of chopped onions. Drizzle margarine over. Salt and pepper. Cover with sliced cheese. Make a second layer but no more. Use a larger dish if more servings are needed. Bake at 350 degrees for 25 - 30 minutes. Cheese makes a marvelous sauce. Make as much or as little of this as you need.

LEMON MUFFINS

½ C soft margarine
½ C sugar
2 eggs - separated
1 C flour
1 tsp baking powder
½ tsp salt
¼ C lemon juice
1 tsp grated lemon peel

Cream margarine and sugar. Add egg yolks and beat until light. Sift dry ingredients together and add alternately with lemon juice. Mix thoroughly but do not over mix. Beat egg whites until soft peaks will form then fold into batter. Add rind. (See helpful hint # 13.) Fill greased muffin tins about ¾ full. Bake at 350 degrees for 20 - 30 minutes. Makes 1 dozen.

CANTALOUPE RINGS

1 cantaloupe
vanilla ice cream

Slice cantaloupe into circles. Remove seeds and cut away rind. Place a scoop of vanilla ice cream in the center. Garnish with a strawberry or mint leaf.

POLYNESIAN CHICKEN SALAD

4 C cooked chicken - chopped
2 C cooked rice
1 C chopped celery
1 can sliced water chestnuts
2 green onions - chopped
1 can (10½ oz) pineapple tidbits - drained
mayonnaise - Hellmann's
green grapes - for garnish

Toss all ingredients. (See helpful hint # 3.) Add enough mayonnaise to moisten. Salt and pepper to taste. Refrigerate until chilled. Serve on a bed of lettuce with a bunch of grapes.

MARINATED CARROTS

5 C cooked carrots - sliced	1 C sugar
2 green onions with tops - chopped	1 can tomato soup
	1 Tbsp Worcestershire
2 ribs celery - chopped	sauce
½ C oil	1 Tbsp lemon juice
¾ C vinegar	1 tsp soy sauce

Cook carrots. (See helpful hint # 17.) Drain and slice. Add chopped onion and celery. Mix remaining ingredients in a sauce pan and boil for 1 - 2 minutes. Pour hot dressing over carrots. Cover and refrigerate. Remove to serving bowl with slotted spoon.

June, 1986 - Etta Mae Neal
Danville, Virginia

PULL APART LOAF

1 bag frozen dinner rolls (24 to pkg)
1 stick melted margarine

Layer frozen rolls in a tube pan or 2 loaf pans. Pour melted margarine over rolls. Cover with a cloth and let rise in a warm place at least 1 hour - half a day is not too long. Bake at 375 degrees for 15 - 20 minutes. Serve loaf on a plate and pull apart sections. (Poppy seeds may be sprinkled over rolls before baking for variation.)

BANANA SPLIT CAKE

CRUST:

1 stick melted butter or margarine
2 C graham cracker crumbs

Mix and press into a 13 x 9" oblong pan.

FILLING:

2 sticks butter - softened
2 eggs
2 C powdered sugar
1 can (15 oz) crushed pineapple - drained
4 bananas
1 carton (8 oz) frozen whipped topping - thawed
1 jar maraschino cherries - chopped
½ C slivered almonds

Cream butter, sugar and eggs until light and fluffy. Pour over crust. Spread crushed pineapple over filling. Next add sliced bananas. Cover with whipped topping. Top with chopped cherries and almonds. Refrigerate several hours before serving. This looks very pretty so take it to the table to serve.

BARBECUED CHICKEN

chicken pieces - skinned

Cook chicken over medium hot coals on a charcoal grill. Baste often with sauce and turn occasionally. Grill 45 minutes - 1 hour. In the event of inclement weather, pour sauce over chicken and bake at 350 degrees for 1 hour.

GOOD and EASY BBQ SAUCE:

½ onion - chopped
1 Tbsp margarine
⅓ bottle chili sauce
⅓ C water
3 Tbsp brown sugar
2 drops Worcestershire sauce
1 Tbsp lemon juice

In a sauce pan sauté onion in butter. Add all other ingredients and cook about 15 minutes or until slightly thickened. If sauce gets too thick, add a little more water. Sauce is also good on spareribs and pork chops.

Libbie T. Crane

NEW POTATOES

Select small new potatoes. Wash and scrape skin with a knife. Boil in salted water until tender. Drain. Serve with butter and fresh snipped chives.

MARINATED VEGETABLES

1 can LeSueur peas -
  drained - reserve ¼ C
1 can french cut beans -
  drained - reserve ¼ C
1 can white shoe peg corn -
  drained
2 stalks celery - chopped

½ C green pepper -
  chopped
1 medium onion - chopped
1 small can sliced mush-
  rooms - drained
1 small jar pimento -
  drained

MARINADE:

1½ C sugar
¾ C vinegar
½ C drained juice from
  vegetables

½ C salad oil
1 tsp paprika
1 tsp salt

Combine marinade ingredients and pour over vegetables. Mix as little as possible. Thoroughly chill. This makes a lot. Keeps well in refrigerator a week or more. Serves 8 - 10.

Blanche McKenney
Farnham, Virginia

CORN MUFFINS

1 C self-rising flour
1 C self-rising cornmeal
½ tsp sugar

2 Tbsp oil
1 egg
1 C milk

Combine flour and meal. Add sugar. Stir in remaining ingredients with a spoon until thoroughly blended. Spoon into greased muffin tins and bake at 400 degrees for 20 - 25 minutes. Makes 12.

BLENDER CHOCOLATE PIE

1 chocolate crumb crust

FILLING:

1 C (6 oz) chocolate chips
1 egg
2 Tbsp sugar
2 Tbsp strong coffee

dash salt
1 tsp vanilla
¾ C boiling water
frozen whipped topping

Place all ingredients in the blender on high speed for 1 minute. Pour into the crumb crust. Refrigerate for 1 hour until set. Smooth on topping. Dust with a little cocoa or shaved chocolate.

Janet Coleman

115

DELUX TURKEY SANDWICHES

"This is good on an especially hot evening."

pita pocket bread
sliced turkey
shredded lettuce
Swiss cheese - grated

alfalfa sprouts
herb dressing
oil and vinegar dressing
(optional)

Spread split pita pockets with **HERB DRESSING:** Ranch Creamy Herb Dressing Mix made with 1 C mayonnaise and 1 C plain yogurt. Fill pocket with sliced turkey and Swiss cheese, shredded lettuce and alfalfa sprouts. Drizzle oil and vinegar dressing on alfalfa sprouts if desired. Helpful hint: salt and pepper turkey slices before making the sandwiches. Make a platter of sandwiches or put all the fixings out and have everyone make their own.

GREEN PEA SALAD

2 cans LeSueur green peas
8 oz sharp cheddar cheese -
grated
1 jar (4 oz) pimento -
drained and chopped
1 C celery - diced
1 can water chestnuts -
chopped

1 - 2 green onions with tops
- chopped
½ **C Hellman's mayonnaise**
salt to taste
fresh parsley for garnish
tomatoes for garnish

Drain peas then further dry on paper towel. Combine with remaining ingredients and gently mix in mayonnaise. Serve on bed of lettuce garnished with wedges of tomato and sprigs of fresh parsley. This makes a big salad but keeps well in refrigerator for several days. Serves 10.

GERMAN CHOCOLATE PIE

1 bar (4 oz) **Baker's German Sweet Chocolate**
⅓ C milk
2 Tbsp sugar
1 pkg (3 oz) **cream cheese** - softened
1 container (8 oz) **whipped topping**
1 graham cracker crumb crust (bought or made with 1 C
   graham cracker crumbs and ½ stick melted butter)

    Melt chocolate with 2 Tbsp milk over low heat. Blend sugar
into cream cheese. Add remainder of milk and melted chocolate.
Stir until smooth. Fold in whipped topping with a wisk until mixed
thoroughly. Pour into crust. Freeze until firm - about 4 hours.

A Baker's Chocolate recipe

NOTES

S
U
M
M
E
R

GAZPACHO

3 C chopped fresh tomatoes	1 tsp fresh basil
1 C chopped green pepper	1 tsp Worcestershire sauce
3 - 4 chopped green onions with tops	½ tsp freshly ground pepper
1 C chopped celery	1 tsp salt
1 C chopped cucumber	1 tsp sugar
6 - 8 large mushrooms - chopped	½ C tarragon vinegar
1 Tbsp fresh parsley	3 Tbsp vegetable oil
1 Tbsp chives	3 C V-8 juice

Coarsely chop vegetables then put in blender for a few seconds. Do one part at a time. Mix all together and chill. Any leftover may be served for lunch or a refreshing snack. Will keep for several days.

CHEESE BREAD

1 egg - beaten	1 Tbsp minced onion
½ C milk	1 C grated sharp cheese - divided
1½ C biscuit mix	
2 Tbsp chopped parsley	¼ C margarine - melted

Combine milk and egg. Add biscuit mix, parsley, onion and ¾ C cheese. Stir until smooth. Pour into a greased 8" cake pan. Sprinkle with remaining cheese and pour melted margarine over top. Bake at 350 degrees for 25 - 30 minutes.

SWISS OMELET ROLL

½ C mayonnaise
2 Tbsp flour
1 C milk
12 eggs - separated
½ tsp salt

⅛ tsp white pepper
1½ C chopped ham
1 C shredded Swiss cheese
¼ C chopped green onion

In a heavy sauce pan combine mayonnaise and flour. Gradually add milk and beaten egg yolks. Cook over low heat stirring constantly until thickened. Remove from heat and cool 15 minutes. Beat egg whites until stiff. Fold mayonnaise mixture and seasonings into egg whites. Line a jelly roll pan with greased waxed paper. Pour in omelet and bake at 425 degrees for 20 minutes. Remove omelet from oven and invert on a towel. Carefully remove waxed paper. Cover evenly with ham, cheese and green onion. Roll from narrow end lifting towel while rolling. (May freeze at this point.) Serve seam side down on a platter. Top with mustard sauce. Arrange fresh vegetables around omelet: cocktail tomatoes, broccoli flowerettes, whole mushrooms. Garnish with parsley or water cress.

SAUCE:

1 C mayonnaise
2 Tbsp prepared mustard

2 Tbsp chopped green onion

Mix and refrigerate.

1982 - Jane Wootton

LEMON ICE-BOX CAKE

1 C graham cracker crumbs
3 Tbsp butter - melted
2 eggs separated
4 Tbsp sugar
1 Tbsp grated lemon rind

½ C fresh lemon juice
¼ tsp almond extract
1 can (14 oz) Eagle Brand condensed milk

Mix cracker crumbs with butter and press into ice cube tray or any pan which will go into the freezer. Chill during remainder of preparation. Beat egg yolks until thickened. Add condensed milk. Add lemon rind and juice. (See helpful hint # 13.) Add almond extract. Stir until blended. Beat egg whites, gradually adding the sugar, until stiff. Fold into lemon mixture. Pour into tray and return to freezer for several hours. Serves 6.

GRILLED HAMBURGERS

BAKED BEANS

COLE SLAW

LETTUCE and TOMATO

❧ OLD FASHIONED PEACH ICE CREAM

GRILLED HAMBURGERS

2 lbs **ground beef** (chuck)
1 envelope **dry onion soup mix**
hamburger rolls
A-1 sauce

Mix the dry soup mix into the ground beef. Form into patties - about 4 - 5 per pound. Cook on charcoal grill over medium hot coals. Freeze unused patties for another time. Serve on warmed or toasted hamburger rolls. A-1 sauce is especially good on these hamburgers.

BAKED BEANS

1 can (medium) **pork and beans**
½ C brown sugar
¼ C tomato catsup
1 Tbsp Worcestershire sauce
1 Tbsp dried onion flakes
1 tsp prepared mustard
salt and pepper to taste
2 slices **bacon**

Mix all ingredients except bacon and pour into a greased baking dish. Cut bacon into small pieces with scissors and spread on top. Bake at 350 degrees for 1 hour.

COLE SLAW

3 - 4 C shredded <u>cabbage</u> (1 small head)
2 medium <u>carrots</u> - grated
2 - 3 green onions - chopped fine
1 tsp celery seed
½ C mayonnaise (Hellmann's)
3 Tbsp <u>sweet pickle relish</u> with vinegar
salt and pepper to taste

Lightly toss vegetables and celery seed together. Add mayonnaise and relish. Stir until mixed thoroughly. Season. Store in refrigerator until serving time.

LETTUCE and TOMATO

Arrange <u>lettuce</u> and sliced <u>tomato</u> on a platter with a dish of mayonnaise to "dress" the hamburgers.

OLD FASHIONED PEACH ICE CREAM

4 C ripe <u>peaches</u> - mashed
½ C sugar
4 eggs
½ pint (1 C) <u>whipping cream</u> - unwhipped
4 tsp vanilla extract
2 cans <u>sweetened condensed milk</u>
¾ C sugar
1½ quarts (6 C) milk

Mix peaches and ½ C sugar and set aside. (Peaches may be pureed in blender but leave some chunks.) Stir frequently. Combine eggs, cream, ¾ C sugar and vanilla in the large mixer bowl and beat. Add condensed milk, peach mixture and milk. Stir to blend. Freeze according to freezer instructions. Store in plastic container in the freezer. Stays creamy. Makes about 4 quarts.

The Words Worth Eating Recipe Collection
At Ukrop's Super Markets

SUMMER

GRILLED HAM STEAK

ham steaks - thick, center cut

SAUCE:

1 Tbsp prepared mustard
1 Tbsp catsup
1 Tbsp honey
2 Tbsp red wine vinegar
2 Tbsp dry sherry

Mix sauce ingredients together. Slash fat edge of ham at 1 inch intervals being careful not to cut into the meat. Grill over hot coals brushing frequently with sauce. This does not take long, about 5 minutes per side, depending on heat of charcoal.

ZUCCHINI BAKE

½ C biscuit mix
¼ C parmesan cheese
1 Tbsp minced parsley
¼ tsp salt
¼ tsp dried oregano flakes
2 eggs
4 Tbsp margarine - melted
2 - 2½ C thinly sliced zucchini
2 - 3 green onions with tops - chopped
fresh ground pepper to taste

Mix biscuit mix, parmesan cheese, herbs and seasonings in a large mixing bowl. In another bowl stir the melted butter with the eggs. Combine the two then gently mix in the zucchini and onion. Spread in a greased Pyrex dish. Bake at 350 degrees for 25 minutes until lightly browned.

CORN on the COB

Shuck ears of corn and trim ends. In a large pot place corn in cold water. Bring to a boil and boil 3 - 5 minutes. Small kernel white corn cooks quicker than the large kernel yellow. Serve with butter, salt and pepper.

LETTUCE and TOMATOES

Slice summer tomatoes on a bed of shredded crisp lettuce. Serve with mayonnaise or salad dressing.

ICE CREAM CAKE

1 half gallon vanilla ice cream
1½ C fine graham cracker crumbs
4 Tbsp sherry (Taylor's Golden) - optional
frozen whipped topping - thawed
grated coconut
fresh strawberries

Soften ice cream. Stir in graham cracker crumbs and sherry. (Children may wish this omitted.) Freeze in a loaf pan. When hard frozen, unmold and ice with whipped topping. Sprinkle with grated coconut and granish with mint leaves and fresh strawberries. Slice to serve. Serves 6 - 8.

Mother, Elizabeth F. Easley

Note: This is also one of my favorite company desserts for summer. Double the recipe and freeze in a tube pan. Use real whipped cream to ice. Decorate with coconut, strawberries and mint leaves. Serve at the table. Serves 12 - 14.

SUMMER

SEA LEG SALAD

FRESH ASPARAGUS

HARD ROLLS

❧ ORANGE CHIFFON CAKE

SEA LEG SALAD

1 lb sea legs
½ lb cooked shrimp
2 C small shell macaroni
3 ribs celery - diced
1 can sliced water chestnuts
1 box frozen green peas

Cook macaroni in lightly salted water. Drain and toss with a few drops of salad oil to keep from being sticky. Combine remaining ingredients.

SALAD DRESSING:

½ C mayonnaise (Hellmann's)
1 tsp dry mustard
1 tsp salt
2 Tbsp cider vinegar
1 Tbsp oil and vinegar dressing (Good Seasons)
3 Tbsp Creamy Herb Dressing (Ranch)
2 Tbsp lemon juice
white pepper to taste

Sprinkle lemon juice and vinegar directly on sea leg mixture. Mix remaining sauce ingredients and add to salad, stirring as little as possible. Chill. Correct seasoning. Add more mayonnaise if needed. Serve on a bed of lettuce with cocktail tomatoes and fresh dill.

FRESH ASPARAGUS

fresh asparagus spears
1 carton (8 oz) plain yogurt
½ C mayonnaise (Hellmann's)
½ tsp curry powder

Trim tough bottom from asparagus. Steam over boiling water for 5 minutes. Plunge immediately into ice water. Drain and chill. Mix yogurt, mayonnaise and curry. Serve over chilled asparagus spears.

HARD ROLLS

Purchase from bakery. Serve at room temperature with softened butter.

ORANGE CHIFFON CAKE

1 orange chiffon cake - bought, made from scratch, or Duncan Hines Orange Supreme Cake Mix. Cut into 4 layers. (See helpful hint # 23.)

ICING:
1 pkg instant vanilla pudding mix
2 C milk
1 can (8 oz) crushed pineapple - drained
½ pint whipping cream - whipped
1 can mandarin oranges - drained

Mix milk with pudding mix and chill slightly. Fold pineapple into the pudding. Whip the cream until stiff and fold into pudding mixture. Ice all four layers then the entire cake. Refrigerate at least 2 hours before serving. Garnish with mandarin oranges. Will keep in the refrigerator for several days.

Mrs. Lawrence G. Wilson, Jr.
Danville, Virginia

SUMMER

SUMMER SALAD

1 C cooked white rice
1 box frozen green peas
½ C Italian dressing
1 small jar green olives -
  sliced
6 - 8 large fresh mushrooms -
  sliced

1 can sliced water chestnuts
2 green onions - chopped
2 C small salad shrimp
mayonnaise - Hellmann's

Cook peas in Italian dressing for 2 - 3 minutes. Cool slightly. Mix rice (See helpful hint # 3.) and remaining ingredients with enough mayonnaise to moisten. Season to taste. Chill until ready to serve. Serves 4.

Beth Fosdal
Middleton, Wisconsin

QUICK and EASY TOMATO ASPIC

1 small box lemon gelatin
2 C V-8 juice
½ tsp onion salt
½ tsp Worcestershire sauce
celery - chopped - optional
green pepper - chopped - optional

Bring 1 C V-8 juice to boil and pour over gelatin. Stir to dissolve. Add 1 C cold V-8, onion salt and Worcestershire sauce. Add celery and pepper if desired. Pour into mold. (See helpful hint # 42.) Refrigerate until firm.

Ellen Dyer Davis
Danville, Virginia

CHEESE and HERB BREAD

2 C warm water (105 degreess - 115 degrees)
2 pkg dry yeast
2 Tbsp sugar
2 tsp salt
2 Tbsp soft butter
½ C plus 1 Tbsp parmesan cheese
1½ Tbsp oregano leaves
4¼ C flour

Sprinkle yeast over water in large bowl of electric mixer. Let stand for few minutes then stir to dissolve yeast. Add sugar, salt, butter, ½ C cheese, oregano and 3 C flour. Beat at low speed until smooth. Scrape bowl and with a wooden spoon gradually add remaining flour. Cover and let rise about 45 minutes in warm place free of drafts. With wooden spoon, stir down batter, and beat with vigor for 25 strokes. Turn into 1½ - 2 qt. greased casserole. Sprinkle 1 Tbsp parmesan cheese on top. Bake at 350 degrees for 50 minutes - 1 hour.

Beverley H. Davis

LEMON BISQUE

1½ C boiling water
1 package (3 oz) lemon flavored gelatin
1 C sugar
1 can (14 oz) sweetened condensed milk - chilled
1 lemon - grated rind and juice
¼ tsp salt
1 C graham cracker crumbs

Dissolve gelatin and sugar in boiling water. Cool and chill to egg-white consistency. Beat milk with mixer until frothy. Beat gelatin until frothy. Add lemon rind, lemon juice and salt to gelatin then beat lemon mixture into milk. Beat until well blended. Put ¾ C cracker crumbs into a sprayed 12 x 8 inch pan. Pour lemon mixture over. Sprinkle the remaining crumbs on the top. Freeze until firm - at least an hour. Serves 6 - 8.

SUMMER

FETTUCCINI with CRAB

¾ lb fettuccini
1 Tbsp cooking oil
1 lb crabmeat or sea legs
½ lb fresh mushrooms - sliced
1 stick margarine
2 cloves garlic
2 Tbsp flour
1 pt half and half
½ C parmesan cheese
salt and white pepper
parsley

Cook fettuccini in lightly salted water. Drain and toss with 1 Tbsp oil to prevent stickiness. Keep warm. Melt margarine in large skillet. Add crushed garlic cloves for few minutes then remove and discard. Sauté mushrooms. Remove and reserve. Stir in flour until smooth. Add half and half. (See helpful hint # 10.) Stir until begins to thicken. Stir in cheese, mushrooms and crab. Season. Continue cooking over medium heat until throughly heated and thickened. Crab may be preheated in the microwave to speed up this step. Add 1 - 2 Tbsp minced fresh parsley saving a few sprigs for garnish. Serve over fettuccini. Serves 4 - 6.

Beth Fosdal
Middleton, Wisconsin

CRISP SLAW

1 large cabbage - shredded
2 - 3 carrots - grated
1 medium onion - minced
1 green pepper - minced

Mix together and place in a plastic container with tight fitting lid.

DRESSING:

1 C cider vinegar
¾ C corn oil
1 C sugar
1 tsp dry mustard
1 tsp celery seed
1 Tbsp salt

Bring to boil in heavy sauce pan. Allow to cool slightly. Pour over vegetables. Do not stir. Cover tightly and refrigerate. Will keep crisp in refrigerator several weeks. Stir before serving.

Anne M. Grigg

SOFT BREAD STICKS - Purchase from bakery section. Serve standing in a tall container with **HERB BUTTER:** Soften 1 stick of butter. Mix in 1 - 2 Tbsp minced fresh herbs - basil, chives, or dill.

SHERBET CAKE

1 pt lime sherbet
1 pt orange sherbet
1 pt raspberry sherbet
1 half gallon butter pecan ice cream
1 carton (8 oz) frozen whipped topping - thawed

In a tube pan spread a layer of softened butter pecan ice cream. Return to freezer until firm. Add a layer of sherbet and another layer of ice cream. Continue in this fashion with the sherbets being separated by ice cream. Freeze until firm. Unmold by holding warm wet towel to outside of tube pan. (There will be a little melt.) Invert on serving plate that can be returned to the freezer. Ice with whipped topping. This a light and colorful dessert for a hot evening.

S
U
M
M
E
R

HEARTY PARMIGIANA

1 lb ground beef - cooked, drained and crumbled
1 medium eggplant - peeled and sliced
1 green pepper - chopped
2 medium zucchini
1 purple onion
2 C extra-thick spaghetti sauce
8 oz grated mozzarella cheese
dried oregano
salt and pepper to taste
parmesan cheese
oil

Cook ground beef until red is gone. Drain and crumble. (See helpful hint # 2.) Prepare vegetables. Put about ½ inch oil in a heavy skillet or electric frypan. Have oil very hot. Drop in eggplant slices and sear on both sides. Remove and drain on paper towels. Turn heat to medium and sauté pepper, zucchini and onion. Remove and drain. In a 7 x 10 inch greased baking dish, make layers as follows: half of the vegetables, half of the ground beef, sprinkle with salt, pepper and oregano, 1 C spaghetti sauce and half of the mozzarella. Make a second similar layer, then top with parmesan cheese. Bake at 350 degrees for 20 - 30 minutes. This can be made ahead and heated at the last minute. Any leftovers are good for lunch. Serves 6 - 8.

TOMATOES - Make individual servings or a large platter of thinly sliced tomatoes on a bed of torn lettuce leaves. Top with a dollop of mayonnaise or salad dressing.

SPOON CORNBREAD

3 C sweet milk - divided
1 C corn meal
1 tsp salt
2 eggs
2 Tbsp melted shortening
2 tsp baking powder

In a heavy sauce pan scald 2 C milk. Add corn meal slowly stirring constantly. Add salt. Cook until thickened. Cool slightly. Add shortening and eggs one at a time. Mix well. Add the remaining cup of milk and then the baking powder. Pour into a 1 quart greased baking dish. Bake at 350 degrees for 40 - 45 minutes or until set and browned on top.

Mother, Elizabeth F. Easley

PEPPERMINT BROWNIES

2 squares unsweetened baking chocolate
½ C butter or margarine
2 eggs - beaten
1 C sugar
¼ tsp peppermint extract
½ C flour
dash salt
½ C chopped nuts

Melt chocolate and butter. Cool slightly. Beat eggs with sugar. Add chocolate mixture. Add peppermint extract. Fold in flour, nuts and salt. Pour into a greased 7 x 11 inch baking pan. Bake at 350 degrees for 20 minutes. Do not over bake. Cool completely.

ICING:

2 Tbsp soft butter
1 C powdered sugar
1 Tbsp cream (or evaporated milk)

1 tsp vanilla
½ tsp peppermint extract
2 drops green food coloring

Mix all ingredients until smooth. Spread on brownie. Refrigerate to chill slightly.

Melt 1 square of semi-sweet baking chocolate with 1 Tbsp butter. Drizzle hot over chilled brownie.

S
U
M
M
E
R

131

CHICKEN with SAUCE

GREEN and GOLD CASSEROLE

TOMATO and CUKE SALAD

MAYO - MUFFINS

ᕗ FRESH FRUIT TORTE

CHICKEN with SAUCE

chicken pieces - skin removed

SAUCE:

1 jar pineapple preserves
1 envelope dry onion soup mix
1 bottle French dressing

Mix and pour over chicken which has been placed in a greased baking dish. Bake at 350 degrees for 1 hour 15 minutes. This chicken is also excellent cooked on the outdoor grill. Baste frequently with the sauce and serve remaining sauce with chicken.

GREEN and GOLD CASSEROLE

3 - 4 medium yellow squash
1 - 2 medium zucchini
1 small onion - sliced
½ C sour cream
½ C mayonnaise
½ C dry bread crumbs
½ C parmesan cheese
salt and pepper to taste

Par boil squash and onion in large pot of lightly salted water. Drain, coursely chop and mash out extra liquid. Stir in remaining ingredients. Season to taste. Pour into a greased casserole dish. Bake at 350 degrees for 30 minutes. Serves 6.

TOMATO and CUKE SALAD

lettuce
tomatoes
cucumbers
oil and vinegar dressing
fresh basil or **dill**
salt and pepper

On a serving platter make a bed of shredded lettuce in the center and whole leaves around the side. Slice fresh tomatoes and cucumbers and arrange on lettuce. Snip fresh herb over, salt and pepper and drizzle salad dressing over all. Refrigerate until serving time. Make as much or as little as you need. This is especially good if you have a garden and can pick everything fresh.

MAYO - MUFFINS

2 C self-rising flour
¼ C mayonnaise
1 C milk
1 tsp sugar

Combine all ingredients and mix well. Spoon into greased muffin tins. Bake at 450 degrees for 10 - 15 minutes. Makes 12.

FRESH FRUIT TORTE

1 roll refrigerator sugar cookie dough
1 pkg (8 oz) cream cheese
3 Tbsp powdered sugar
½ C orange marmalade
fresh fruit - strawberries, kiwi, bananas, pineapple,
    grapes, etc.

Slice cookie dough and allow to soften. Press into a lightly greased quiche pan, pie plate or pizza pan to form a crust. Bake at 375 degrees for 8 - 10 minutes or until brown. Allow to cool. Blend cream cheese and powdered sugar. Spread over cookie crust. Arrange fruit in single layer circles in any combination desired. Heat marmalade and spoon over fruit. May refrigerate or serve immediately. Do not make too far ahead as crust gets soggy. One cookie roll will make 2 pie-size crusts. The second may be wrapped and frozen for another time.

TARRAGON CHICKEN SALAD

BUTTER BEANS

LIME - GRAPE GELATIN MOLD

HAM BISCUITS

MACAROON ICE CREAM DESSERT

TARRAGON CHICKEN SALAD

6 chicken breasts
½ C mayonnaise - Hellman's
½ C sour cream
1 C chopped celery
¼ C golden raisins
1 pkg slivered almonds
2 Tbsp fresh tarragon (or 2 tsp dried)
salt and pepper
green grapes

Cook chicken in lightly salted water until tender. Discard skin and cut into chunks. Cool. Mix mayonnaise and sour cream together then add to chicken. Stir in remaining ingredients and season. Refrigerate. Serve on a bed of lettuce with a bunch of green grapes. Serves 4 - 6.

BUTTER BEANS

Shell and wash new butter beans (baby limas). Cook in lightly salted water until tender (about 30 - 45 minutes). Drain. Add butter and salt.

LIME - GRAPE GELATIN MOLD

1 (3 oz) pkg lime flavored gelatin
¼ C freshly squeezed lime juice
1 C small green seedless grapes
2 ½ Tbsp mayonnaise
⅓ C sour cream
salt and sugar to taste

Prepare gelatin according to package directions substituting the lime juice for part of water. Fold in grapes. Pour into molds and chill until firm. Mix mayonnaise and sour cream. A dash of salt and sugar may be added. Place a dollop of dressing on each serving. Serves 4.

Janet Coleman

HAM BISCUITS

Prepare your favorite biscuits or rolls. Butter and fill with sliced ham. Serve warm.

MACAROON ICE CREAM DESSERT

½ gal coffee ice cream
½ lbs almond macaroons
rum or sherry (Taylor's Golden)
½ pt whipped cream or frozen whipped topping
1 pkg slivered almonds - toasted

Remove ice cream from freezer to soften. Crumble macaroons in a 3 quart bowl. Sprinkle rum or sherry over macaroons. Spread softened ice cream over macaroons then cover with whipped cream. Sprinkle with toasted almonds. Toast almonds by placing them in a flat pan under the broiler for a few minutes until they have browned - watch closely. Place dessert in freezer until firm. Remove from freezer a short while before serving. Serves 8.

Betty Rose Sexton
1984

SUMMER

FLOUNDER FILLETS a la FLORENTINE

6 Tbsp melted butter or
  margarine
½ C herb-seasoned stuffing
3 lbs flounder fillets
2 Tbsp butter or margarine
salt and pepper
2 tsp lemon juice
1 tsp Worcestershire sauce

¼ C white wine
1 pkg (12 oz) frozen spinach
  soufflé - thawed
½ C grated parmesan
  cheese
1 jar (2½ oz) sliced mushrooms - drained

Toss melted butter with stuffing. Set aside. Pat flounder fillets dry. Arrange in a single layer in a greased 9 x 13 inch shallow baking dish. Dot with butter. Salt and pepper. Mix lemon juice, Worcestershire and wine and pour over. Spread spinach soufflé over fillets. Top with cheese, mushrooms and the reserved stuffing. Bake at 375 degrees for about 25 minutes or until fish flakes easily when tested with a fork. Serves 6 - 8.

Phyllis Galanti

BAKED TOMATOES - Cut stem end tops from medium size firm tomatoes. Drizzle melted butter over and sprinkle generously with salt, pepper and dried oregano. Place in greased muffin tins (See helpful hint # 35.) and bake at 350 degrees for 20 minutes. Pour small amount of water in unused muffin wells.

REFRIGERATOR BISCUITS - A can of flakey biscuits cooked as package directs.

SQUASH CASSEROLE

4 medium <u>yellow squash</u>
3 Tbsp margarine
2 Tbsp chopped onion
3 Tbsp chopped <u>pepper</u>
2 hard cooked <u>eggs</u> - sliced
2 pieces <u>toast</u> - cubed
1½ tsp salt
⅛ tsp pepper
2 Tbsp bacon drippings
½ C sharp cheese - grated

Slice squash and par boil until just tender or cook 2 minutes in a pressure cooker. Drain. Sauté onion and pepper in margarine until golden. Combine salt, pepper, sliced eggs, bread cubes and bacon drippings. Mix with squash. Place in a greased baking dish. Bake at 350 degrees for 45 minutes. Top with grated cheese and bake 15 minutes longer. This may be made up early in the day and baked at supper time. Serves 6.

Phyllis Galanti

FUDGE SUNDAE PIE

1 C evaporated milk
6 oz package <u>semi-sweet chocolate bits</u>
1 C <u>mini-marshmallows</u>
¼ tsp salt
1 qt <u>vanilla ice cream</u>
<u>vanilla wafers</u>
½ C <u>pecan pieces</u>

Remove ice cream from freezer to soften. In a heavy sauce pan, stir milk, marshmallows and chocolate bits over medium heat until melted and thickened. Add salt. Set aside to cool. Line bottom and sides of a 9" pie pan with vanilla wafers. Spoon half the ice cream over the wafers. Cover with half the chocolate sauce. Repeat with the remaining ice cream and chocolate sauce. Sprinkle pecans over top. Freeze until firm - about 3 hours. So rich it will serve 8 - 10.

Phyllis Galanti

GRILLED LONDON BROIL - BURGUNDY SAUCE

MUSTARD POTATOES

❧ LAYERED SALAD

BAKERY LOAF

LIBBIE'S FRUIT COBBLER

LONDON BROIL

2 lb <u>London Broil</u> - Grill over hot charcoal about 8 minutes per side or to desired doneness.

BURGUNDY SAUCE:

2 sticks margarine
12 large <u>mushrooms</u> - sliced
3 - 4 green onions with tops - chopped
2 Tbsp Worcestershire sauce

1 Tbsp cornstarch
½ C <u>burgundy wine</u>
<u>Kitchen Bouquet</u> for color
3 - 4 sprigs fresh parsley - snipped

Melt margarine in sauce pan and sauté mushrooms and onions serveral minutes. Add Worcestershire. Stir cornstarch into burgundy until smooth then add, stirring constantly until thickened. Add Kitchen Bouquet to make rich brown color. Add parsley last. Remove from heat and serve with thinly sliced London Broil. Serves 6.

MUSTARD POTATOES

1½ lb <u>new red potatoes</u>
2 yellow onions - optional
½ C Dijon mustard
2 Tbsp red wine vinegar

1 tsp sugar
salt and freshly ground pepper

Slice potatoes into ½ inch slices. Drop into rapidly boiling salted water for about 5 minutes. Rinse under cold water and drain. Slice onions into ½ inch rings; add to potatoes. Mix mustard, vinegar and sugar; toss gently with potatoes. Place on the grill in a wire basket or wrapped in aluminum foil for about 10 minutes per side. Season to taste. Serves 4 - 6.

LAYERED SALAD

lettuce
spinach
2 stalks celery - diced
¼ C green pepper - diced
½ medium red onion - thinly sliced
2 slices bacon - cooked and crumbled
1 can sliced water chestnuts - drained
1 C mayonnaise - Hellmann's
½ C sharp cheese - grated

In a salad bowl break lettuce and spinach into bite size pieces. Layer the next 5 ingredients. Spread mayonnaise over top completely covering and "sealing" edges. Sprinkle with cheese. Cover with plastic wrap and refrigerate at least 4 hours and up to 24 hours before serving.

BAKERY LOAF BREAD

Serve a crusty loaf of bakery bread with soft butter.

LIBBIE'S FRUIT COBBLER

1 C self-rising flour
1 C sugar
1 C milk
1 stick butter or margarine
2 cups blackberries or peaches
¼ C sugar
dash nutmeg

Melt butter. Add to sugar, milk and flour. Pour into a greased square Pyrex dish. Prepare fruit: wash and drain berries or peel and cut up peaches. Spread fruit evenly over batter. Sprinkle with ¼ C sugar and nutmeg. Bake at 350 degrees for 45 minutes - 1 hour. Serves 6.

Libbie T. Crane

S
U
M
M
E
R

TERIYAKI FLANK STEAK

NEW POTATOES

TOSSED GREEN SALAD

BUTTERMILK MUFFINS

BLACKBERRY COBBLER

TERIYAKI FLANK STEAK - GRILLED

1½ lb <u>flank steak</u>
2 Tbsp <u>olive oil</u>
1 tsp garlic salt
2 Tbsp soy sauce
2 Tbsp lemon juice
3 Tbsp <u>honey</u>

Score steak diagonally, across the grain with a sharp knife on both sides. Rub 1 Tbsp olive oil and ½ tsp garlic salt on each side of steak. Mix soy sauce, lemon juice and honey. Pour over steak and allow to stand until cooking time. Flank steak needs to be cooked very fast over very hot coals about 5 minutes per side or to desired doneness. Slice very thin on a 45 degree angle. Pour remaining sauce over sliced meat. Serves 6.

NEW POTATOES

Boil <u>new potatoes</u> in salted water until tender. Toss with butter, salt, pepper and fresh snipped parsley.

TOSSED GREEN SALAD

Top a bed of shredded <u>lettuce</u> with a variety of raw summer vegetables - <u>tomatoes, cucumbers, small squash, onions</u> and <u>peppers</u>. Salt and pepper and cover in a favorite dressing.

BUTTERMILK MUFFINS

1 C buttermilk
¼ tsp soda
1 C self-rising flour
1 egg - beaten

Combine buttermilk and soda. Add flour, stirring until smooth. Stir in egg. Spoon into greased muffin tins. Bake at 425 degrees for 30 - 40 minutes.

BLACKBERRY COBBLER

pie crust for a 2 crust deep dish pie
3 - 4 C blackberries
1½ - 2 C sugar
1 - 2 Tbsp flour
dash salt
4 - 6 Tbsp margarine
dash nutmeg

Roll bottom crust large enough to fall well over edges of a greased Pyrex baking dish - either square or oblong. Gently rinse berries under cool water and drain. Add sugar, flour and salt. Stir as little as possible to mix. Pour into pie crust. Dot with margarine and a generous sprinkling of nutmeg. Roll top crust to cover. Fold and pinch edges to seal. Prick top with a fork. Preheat oven to 500 degrees. Put cobbler in oven and turn temperature to 350 degrees immediately. Bake about 1 hour. *"Nutmeg is the secret."*

My Aunt, Margaret F. Hankins

SUMMER

NOTES

AUTUMN

MAIN DISHES

Whole Beef Tenderloin • Fifteen-Minute Stroganoff • Cheese Soufflé • Chicken and Rice Casserole • Smoked Sausage • Salmon Cakes • Pork Roast • Pork Chops • Chicken and Wild Rice • Freda's Dish • Marinated Pork Tenderloin • Can-Can Chicken • Tarragon Chicken • Super Chicken Casserole • Seafood Casserole • Burger 'N Beans • Steak and Gravy • Ham Steaks • Scallops Au Gratin • Baked Spaghetti

VEGETABLES

Rice Casserole • Noodles • Tomato Soup • Broccoli with Lemon Butter • Pennsylvania Red Cabbage • Broccoli with Cheese • Tomato Slices • Asparagus Casserole • Baked Sweet Potato • Black-Eyed Peas • Baked Tomatoes • Broccoli • Buttered Peas • Sweet Potato Pudding • French-Cut Green Beans • Butter Beans • Corn Pudding • Potato Casserole • Brussel Sprouts • Pineapple Bake • Baked Acorn Squash • Green Bean Casserole

SALADS

Hearts of Palm • Lettuce • Lettuce and Pea • Waldorf • Hearty Tossed • Pink Artic • Orange-Pineapple • Tossed • Apple Slaw • Tomato Delight

BREADS

Ida's Sally Lunn • Bakery Loaf with Herb Butter • Rolls • Caraway Seed • Corn Bread • Apple Yorkshire Pudding • Cheese Bread • Buttermilk Muffins • Fresh Apple Muffins • Cheese Spoon Bread • Quick Little Loaf • Cheese Loaf • Poppy Seed Biscuits • Light Muffins

DESSERTS

Burgundy Pears • Mocha Brownie Cake • Yummy Apple Cobbler • Pecan Pie • Cran-Apple Crunch • Chewy Brownies • Damson Pie • Brown Sugar Pie • Butterscotch Brownies • Gingerbread with Raisin Sauce • Coconut Pie • Toffee Squares • Apple Cobbler • Oatmeal Squares • Beth's Apple Pie • Caramel Chocolate Squares • Coconut Macaroons • Nutmeg Pound Cake • Black Forest Cake • Pistachio Pie

BEEF TENDERLOIN

1 whole beef tenderloin - Have butcher trim and tie.

Preheat oven to 500 degrees. Place tenderloin on a rack and into oven. (See helpful hint # 11.) Immediately reduce heat to 350 degrees and cook 1 hour. Remove from oven and allow to stand 5 minutes before slicing. It should be medium rare. One tenderloin serves 8 adults.

RICE CASSEROLE

1 C Uncle Ben's converted rice
2 cans beef consomme
½ soup can water
1 C chopped celery
1 stick margarine
paprika

In greased oblong baking dish put rice, liquids and celery. Dot with margarine and sprinkle with paprika. Cook at 350 degrees for 1 hour.

HEARTS of PALM SALAD

lettuces - endive, bib, iceberg
1 can hearts of palm - drained
1 can artichoke hearts - drained and quartered
1 can sliced water chestnuts - drained
1 can bean sprouts - drained
1 purple onion - sliced in rings
oil and vinegar dressing

Break lettuces up into bite-size pieces. Toss with salad dressing. Arrange remaining ingredients on top of lettuce. Drizzle additional dressing over all. Serve immediately.

IDA'S SALLY LUNN

"Of all the Sally Lunns, this is my favorite."

1 cake of yeast or 1 pkg dry
¼ C warm water (105 degrees - 115 degrees)
2 eggs - room temperature
½ C sugar
5 Tbsp corn oil
1 tsp salt
1 C warm milk
4 C flour

Mix yeast in warm water until dissolved. Set aside. In large mixer bowl beat eggs and sugar together. Add remaining ingredients in the order given. Then slowly add yeast mixture. Mix only until blended. Allow dough to rise in bowl about 2 hours. (See helpful hint # 32.) Stir down with a wooden spoon and pour into a greased tube pan. Allow to rise again. Bake at 350 degrees for 30 - 35 minutes.

1975 - Ida Latham

BURGUNDY PEARS

2 lbs small firm pears
1½ C sugar
1 tsp cinnamon
1 C burgundy wine

Peel pears but leave whole. Leave stem on and cut flat at blossom end so pear will stand up when served. In a heavy sauce pan bring the sugar and ¾ C water just to a boil. Reduce heat. Add pears gently. Cover and simmer 15 minutes. Add the burgundy and simmer 15 minutes uncovered. Transfer pears to a shallow dish. Boil down the juice until it is the consistency of light syrup. Pour over pears. Cover with plastic wrap and thoroughly chill. Serve a pear per person. Children enjoy this - the wine taste is not strong.

A
U
T
U
M
N

FIFTEEN - MINUTE STROGANOFF

NOODLES

LETTUCE SALAD

BAKERY LOAF - HERB BUTTER

&❧ MOCHA BROWNIE CAKE

FIFTEEN - MINUTE STROGANOFF

2 C <u>cooked beef</u> (leftover) - cut in thin strips
2 Tbsp flour
3 Tbsp margarine
2 onions - thinly sliced
6 - 8 large <u>fresh mushrooms</u> - sliced
1 C <u>consomme</u>
1 Tbsp plus 1 tsp <u>tomato paste</u>
1 tsp Worcestershire sauce
1 C sour cream
salt and pepper

Flour beef lightly, reserving any remaining flour. Melt margarine in a large skillet. Sauté onion and mushrooms until golden; add meat and continue to cook until thoroughly heated. Remove and reserve. Stir remaining flour into pan drippings. Add the consomme, tomato paste, Worcestershire and seasonings. Stir and cook until smooth and thickened. Return meat mixture to pan and cook until heated. Just before serving stir in sour cream. Serve over noodles. Serves 4.

NOODLES - medium <u>flat noodles</u> cooked according to package directions.

LETTUCE SALAD

Slice a <u>hard head of lettuce</u> into wedges. A blue cheese or thousand island <u>salad dressing</u> is a good accompaniment to this meal.

148

BAKERY LOAF - HERB BUTTER

Warm a big <u>crusty loaf</u> of bread and serve with **HERB BUTTER:** 1 softened stick of butter plus 1 Tbsp minced fresh chives or 1½ tsp dried.

MOCHA BROWNIE CAKE

1 pkg <u>fudge brownie mix</u>
½ C <u>chopped pecans</u>
1 C <u>whipping cream</u>
3½ Tbsp brown sugar
2 tsp <u>instant coffee granules</u>

Make brownie as package directs using 2 eggs for cake-like texture. Add ½ C pecans to brownie mix. Divide batter between 2 cake pans - 8 or 9 inch - which have been greased and lined with waxed paper. Bake at 350 degrees for 15 - 18 minutes. Cool for 5 - 10 minutes then remove from pans and cool completely. Layers will be thin. Whip cream until it begins to stiffen then gradually add sugar and coffee. Continue beating until stiff. Spread whipped cream mixture between the brownie layers then over entire cake. Additional pecans may be used to garnish if desired. Refrigerate until serving time.

TOMATO SOUP

CHEESE SOUFFLÉ

BROCCOLI with LEMON BUTTER

YUMMY APPLE COBBLER

TOMATO SOUP

2 cans <u>beef consomme</u>   celery stalks
1 large <u>can</u> (46 oz) V-8 juice
1 Tbsp Worcestershire
  sauce

Combine all except celery in a heavy sauce pan. Heat thoroughly - do not boil. Serve in mugs with stalk of celery. Serves 6.

CHEESE SOUFFLÉ

8 oz <u>sharp cheese</u> - cut into   4 eggs
  chunks   2 C milk
10 slices <u>white bread</u> - cut   1 tsp salt
  off crusts   ½ tsp dry mustard
2½ Tbsp butter or marga-
  rine

Divide the ingredients in half and process in the blender on high speed. Pour mixture into a greased uncovered 1½ quart round casserole. Bake at 350 for 50 - 60 minutes. This can be prepared ahead and kept in refrigerator until baking time. Serves 6.

The Words Worth Eating Recipe Collection
Ukrop's Super Market

BROCCOLI with LEMON BUTTER

2 bunches <u>broccoli</u>   1 stick butter
1 lemon - juiced

Wash and trim broccoli. Steam over boiling water for 5 minutes. Transfer to a serving dish. Salt. Melt butter. Stir in lemon juice and drizzle over hot broccoli. Serves 4.

150

YUMMY APPLE COBBLER

1 stick margarine
2 C sugar
3 C water
1½ C self-rising flour
½ C shortening
⅓ C milk
2 C finely chopped <u>apples</u> - golden delicious
1 tsp cinnamon
½ tsp allspice
nutmeg - generous dash
dash salt

    Melt margarine in a 13x9" baking dish in a 350 degree oven. In a sauce pan heat sugar and water until sugar dissolves. Cut shortening into flour then stir in milk with a fork until moistened. Knead on a floured surface until smooth. Roll into a large rectangle about ¼ inch thick. Sprinkle spices over apples then spread evenly over dough. Roll jelly-roll fashion. Moisten edges to seal. Cut in slices about ½ inch thick. Place in dish with margarine. Pour sugar syrup over all. This looks like too much liquid but it isn't. Preparation time is about 20 - 25 minutes and well worth it. Bake at 350 degrees for about 1 hour.

NOTES

AUTUMN

CHICKEN and RICE CASSEROLE

LETTUCE and PEA SALAD

&. ROLLS

PECAN PIE

CHICKEN and RICE CASSEROLE

2 C cooked chicken chunks
3 C cooked rice
2 cans cream of mushroom soup
2 green peppers - cut in strips
1 large onion - chopped
1 soup can milk
salt and pepper to taste

Mix all ingredients and season. Pour into a greased 2 quart casserole. Bake at 325 degrees for about 30 minutes. May be made ahead. Serves 4 - 6.

Claudia C. Easley
Danville, Virginia

LETTUCE and PEA SALAD

1 medium head of lettuce
2 cans LeSueur peas - drained
1 red onion - thinly sliced and separated
1 pt mayonnaise
1 C parmesan cheese

Tear lettuce into bite-size pieces. Place in a 3 quart oblong glass dish. Layer the peas and onions on top. Spread mayonnaise on top and seal edges. Sprinkle with parmesan cheese. May be made ahead and kept in the refrigerator until serving time. Serves 4 - 6.

Claudia C. Easley
Danville, Virginia

ROLLS

1 C shortening
½ C sugar and 2 tsp sugar
1 C boiling water
2 pkg dry yeast or yeast cakes
2 eggs - well beaten
6 C flour - measure before sifting
1 Tbsp salt

Cream shortening with ½ C sugar. Pour boiling water over and cool. Dissolve yeast and 2 tsp sugar in 1 C tap water - about 110 degrees. Set aside to "work". Beat eggs in large bowl of mixer. Add salt and cooled shortening mixture. Spoon flour lighly into measuring cup. Do not pack. Sift. Gradually combine flour and liquids until smooth. Change to dough hooks if needed. Cover with buttered waxed paper and refrigerate overnight. Next day roll out on floured surface. Cut large circles. Rub melted butter on both sides. Fold over envelope style. Place on greased baking sheet. Cover with towel and allow to rise about 1 hour. Bake at 425 degrees for 10 - 12 minutes. Makes 4 - 5 dozen. Freeze in 1 meal packages. Dough will keep 3 - 4 days in refrigerator.

Mother, Elizabeth F. Easley

PECAN PIE

3 eggs
1 Tbsp butter - melted
1 C light corn syrup
1 C sugar
1 Tbsp flour
½ tsp vanilla
1 C pecan halves
1 unbaked 9 inch pie crust

Beat eggs with a wisk until frothy. Add melted butter, corn syrup and vanilla to eggs. Combine sugar and flour. Blend well into egg mixture. Arrange pecan halves in the bottom of the pie crust. Pour mixture over pecans and let stand until they rise to the surface. Bake at 350 degrees for 45 minutes or until set.

Mother, Elizabeth F. Easley

AUTUMN

153

SMOKED SAUSAGE

1 lb smoked sausage - Hillshire Farms

Cut sausage into 3 - 4 inch lengths. Place on a rack in a foil lined pan. Cook in a 350 degree oven for about 30 minutes. Serve on platter with cabbage. Serves 4 - 6.

PENNSYLVANIA RED CABBAGE

2 Tbsp bacon drippings or margarine
4 C shredded red cabbage (1 small head)
2 C chopped unpared golden delicious apples
¼ C brown sugar
¼ C water
¼ C cider vinegar
1¼ tsp salt
½ tsp caraway seed
dash pepper

Coarsely shred cabbage. Heat bacon drippings in a large skillet with a top or an electric frying pan. Stir in sugar, vinegar and water. Add cabbage and apples. Sprinkle caraway seeds, salt and pepper over. Cover and simmer 20 -30 minutes just until crisp tender. Stir occasionally. Serve on a platter surrounded by sausage. Serves 6.

Anne M. Grigg

154

CARAWAY SEED BREAD

3½ C sifted flour
⅔ C sugar
1 Tbsp baking powder
1 tsp baking soda
1 tsp salt
1 C raisins
1 Tbsp caraway seeds
2 eggs - beaten
1½ C buttermilk
2 Tbsp melted butter

Sift dry ingredients together in large mixing bowl. Stir in raisins and caraway seeds. Stir together beaten eggs, buttermilk and melted butter. Add to dry ingredients and mix by hand until blended. Pour into a greased and floured loaf pan. Bake at 375 degrees for 1 hour.

CRAN-APPLE CRUNCH

4 medium golden delicious apples
1 tsp cinnamon
1 can (16 oz) whole cranberry sauce
1 C uncooked quick rolled oats
½ C flour
1 C brown sugar
½ C butter

Peel apples and slice thin. Arrange in a greased oblong baking dish. Sprinkle with cinnamon. Spoon cranberry sauce over apples. Mix oatmeal, flour and sugar. Cut in butter until evenly mixed and crumbly. Spread over cranberry layer. Bake at 350 degrees for 30 - 40 minutes. Serve plain or with ice cream or whipped topping. Serves 8.

AUTUMN

SALMON CAKES

1 **can salmon** - drained
  and fork flaked
1 tsp grated onion
1 C **mashed potatoes** (left-
  over or instant)

1 **egg - beaten**
1 **Tbsp flour**
6 **crackers** - broken into
  fine crumbs

Mix all ingredients together. Shape into patties. Fry in small amount of oil over medium heat until browned - about 10 - 15 minutes. Serves 4.

Miriam Gregory
Java, Virginia

BROCCOLI with CHEESE

Wash and trim 2 bunches broccoli. Steam over boiling water for 5 minutes. Drain and transfer to serving dish. Salt. Melt Cheese Whiz in the microwave or sauce pan. Pour over broccoli. Serve immediately.

TOMATO SLICES

3 - 4 medium tomatoes
2 Tbsp margarine
2 Tbsp parmesan cheese
chopped fresh chives or dried

Melt margarine in shallow dish. Make single layer of thick slices of unpeeled tomatoes. Sprinkle with cheese, chives, salt and pepper. Place under the broiler for 2 - 3 minutes or until cheese begins to brown. Serve warm. Serves 4.

CORN BREAD

1 C self-rising corn meal
¼ C flour - regular
1 Tbsp sugar
1 egg - beaten
1 C buttermilk
2 Tbsp oil

Heat an 8 inch iron skillet (or round casserole) with the oil in 400 degree oven. Sift dry ingredients together. Mix with egg and buttermilk. Pour into hot skillet and place immediately into oven. Bake 15 - 20 minutes. Turn out on a plate. Cut in wedges. Serve with lots of butter.

Miriam Gregory
Java, Virginia

CHEWY BROWNIES

7 Tbsp butter or margarine - melted
1 C sugar
5 Tbsp cocoa
1 C flour
1 tsp vanilla
2 eggs
⅓ tsp baking powder
½ C chopped nuts
dash salt

Mix sugar and cocoa. Add melted butter. Stir in other ingredients. Pour into a greased square pan. Bake at 325 degrees for 20 - 25 minutes. Cool about 10 minutes before cutting.

Miriam Gregory
Java, Virginia

AUTUMN

157

PORK ROAST

pork roast - boneless, trimmed and tied
2 Tbsp ground ginger
¼ C soy sauce

Pour soy sauce over pork roast. Rub ground ginger over all. Place on a rack in a pan with water to cover bottom. Place in a 325 degree oven for about 30 minutes per pound. Remove from oven and let rest for 5 minutes before slicing.

APPLE YORKSHIRE PUDDING

6 Tbsp margarine
½ C light brown sugar
1½ tsp cinnamon
2½ C peeled and sliced apples
1½ C sifted flour
¾ tsp salt
3 eggs
1½ C milk

Melt margarine in oblong baking dish. Sprinkle brown sugar and cinnamon evenly over margarine. Arrange apples over sugar. Sift flour and salt together. Beat eggs until light. Add flour and ½ C milk to eggs until well blended. Gradually add the last cup of milk. Beat until smooth. Gently pour over apples. Bake at 450 degrees for 25 - 30 minutes. Cut in squares and serve at once. Serves 6.

ASPARAGUS CASSEROLE

2 cans cut asparagus
3 Tbsp margarine
3 Tbsp flour
¾ C milk
¼ C liquid from asparagus
salt and pepper
1 can sliced water chestnuts
1 C buttered bread crumbs
1 C grated sharp cheese

Drain asparagus reserving ¼ C liquid. Make a white sauce: Melt margarine in heavy sauce pan, stir in flour until smooth, stir in milk and cook until thickened then add reserved liquid. Place asparagus in a greased shallow baking dish. Spread water chestnuts on top. Salt and pepper. Pour white sauce over. Top with bread crumbs and grated cheese. Place in a 350 degree oven until bubbly hot and cheese melts - about 15 - 20 minutes. Serves 6.

BAKED SWEET POTATOES

Choose medium sized sweet potatoes allowing one per person. Wash, pat dry, prick skin with a fork and rub with margarine or bacon drippings. Bake at 350 degrees for 1 hour or until soft. Split and fill with a big chunk of butter. Serve immediately.

DAMSON PIE

1 unbaked pie crust
Prick pie crust and bake at 450 degrees for 10 minutes.

FILLING:

½ C butter - melted
½ C sugar
1 C damson jam
3 eggs - beaten
½ tsp vanilla

Beat eggs until frothy. Add sugar, damson jam, melted butter and vanilla. Pour into pie crust. Bake at 325 degrees for 40 minutes.

PORK CHOPS

center cut pork chops -
  trim fat
flour

salt and pepper
cooking oil

Dredge pork chops in flour to which salt and pepper have been generously added. Heat oil in an electric skillet or dutch oven. Fry pork chops quickly until all the pink is gone and slightly browned. Do not over cook. Remove and drain all but 1 Tbsp oil. Return pork chops and add ½ - ¾ C water. Steam for about 30 minutes. Add more water, a little at a time, if needed. Correct seasoning. It makes its own gravy.

BLACK-EYED PEAS

Cook fresh black-eyed peas in water with a piece of ham or smoked bacon for about 1 hour. If canned peas are used, season with bacon drippings. Cook until tender but not mushy.

BAKED TOMATOES

1 large can stewed toma-
  toes
1 small yellow onion -
  chopped
3 - 4 biscuits or stale slices
  of bread

½ - ¾ C sugar
salt and pepper
2 Tbsp margarine

Empty tomatoes in mixing bowl and cut up large pieces. Add onion, crumbled bread, sugar and seasonings. Stir to moisten bread. Melt butter in a greased casserole. Pour in tomatoes and bake 1 hour at 350 degrees.

CORN BREAD

1 C self-rising flour
1 C self-rising yellow corn meal
½ tsp salt
2 Tbsp cooking oil
1 egg
½ tsp sugar
1 C buttermilk

Combine flour, meal and salt. Make a well and pour in oil. Stir with a fork. Make another well. Break in egg, add sugar and stir mixture with a fork. Add milk. Stir until well blended. Bake in a greased baking dish at 400 degrees for 20 - 25 minutes. Serve very hot with lots of butter.

BROWN SUGAR PIE

1 unbaked 9" pie crust
3 eggs
¾ box (1½ C) brown sugar - packed
3 Tbsp milk
½ tsp baking powder
2 tsp flour
½ stick melted butter
1 tsp vanilla
butter pecan ice cream - optional

Beat eggs. Add sugar, milk, baking powder and flour then melted butter and vanilla. Stir as little as possible to mix well. Pour into pie crust. Bake at 325 degrees until "set" - about 45 minutes to 1 hour. This pie is good by itself or with butter pecan ice cream.

1963 - Margaret D. Powell
Danville, Virginia

AUTUMN

CHICKEN with WILD RICE

1 box Uncle Ben's long grain and wild rice
2 C chicken broth - canned
3 Tbsp butter or margarine
salt and pepper to taste
1 can (3 oz) sliced mushrooms
6 chicken breasts - boned and skinned
½ pkg dry onion soup mix
1 can cream of mushroom soup
paprika

Sprinkle the rice in a greased oblong baking dish. Pour chicken broth over. Dot with butter. Add mushrooms. Place chicken breasts on rice. Sprinkle with the dried onion soup mix. Salt and pepper. (This is salty so use less salt than usual.) Dilute mushroom soup with enough water to make a thick gravy consistency. Spoon over each breast. Sprinkle the seasoning packet from the rice over all and "dust" with paprika. Cook uncovered at 350 degrees for 1 hour. Cover and cook another 30 minutes. Serves 6.

BROCCOLI

Wash and trim fresh broccoli stalks and steam over boiling water 5 minutes. Drain and pour melted butter over. Salt to taste. Serve immediately.

WALDORF SALAD

2 golden delicious apples - medium size
2 red delicious apples - medium size
½ C celery - chopped fine
½ C **walnut pieces**
½ C **golden raisins**
mayonnaise - Hellmann's

Core and chop apples - do not peel. Add remaining ingredients and enough mayonnaise to moisten. Refrigerate until serving time. Garnish with parsley sprigs. Serves 6.

SOUR DOUGH ROLLS - Buy sour dough rolls. Wrap in aluminum foil to heat. Serve with lots of butter.

BUTTERSCOTCH BROWNIES

2 C flour
1 box (2 C) brown sugar
1 tsp baking powder
¼ tsp soda
½ tsp salt
⅔ C butter - melted
2 eggs
2 tsp vanilla
1 C chopped pecans

Mix dry ingredients thoroughly in large bowl of electric mixer. Break up lumps of brown sugar by hand if necessary. Add melted butter, eggs, vanilla and pecans. Mix well. Pour into a greased 13 x 9 x 2 inch pan. Bake at 350 degrees for 30 minutes. Do not overbake. Allow to cool in pan before cutting into squares. Pass around a plate of brownies for dessert.

Mother, Elizabeth F. Easley

FREDA'S DISH

HEARTY TOSSED SALAD

CHEESE BREAD

GINGERBREAD with RAISIN SAUCE

FREDA'S DISH

1 lb ground beef
1 small onion
1 C macaroni

1 can tomato soup
1 C sharp cheese - grated

Brown beef and onion. Drain. Cook macaroni in lightly salted water until almost done. Drain. Mix beef, onions, macaroni, soup and ½ C of the grated cheese. Put in a greased casserole and top with remaining cheese. Bake at 350 degrees for about 40 minutes. Serves 4.

"Everyone loves this!"
Burrell Stultz

HEARTY TOSSED SALAD

Choose a variety of greens and raw vegetables to combine in a salad. Broccoli and cauliflower flowerettes and tiny yellow squash sliced make nice additions. For winter tomatoes: scoop out the seeds and cut the firmer outer edge in strips. Toss with an oil and vinegar dressing.

CHEESE BREAD

½ C milk
1 egg - beaten
1½ C biscuit mix
2 Tbsp chopped parsley

1 Tbsp minced onion
1 C grated sharp cheese - divided
¼ C margarine - melted

Combine egg and milk. Add biscuit mix, parsley, onion and ½ C cheese. Pour into an 8 or 9 inch cake layer pan. Sprinkle with reserved ½ C cheese and pour melted margarine over all. Bake at 350 degrees for 25 minutes. Turn out on serving plate and cut into wedges. Serve with softened butter.

GINGERBREAD - RAISIN SAUCE

1 pkg gingerbread mix

Prepare as package directs.

RAISIN SAUCE:

1 C raisins
1 C sugar
1 stick margarine
½ tsp soda
½ tsp vanilla
1 Tbsp Karo syrup
¼ C buttermilk

Soak raisins in warm water while preparing sauce. In a heavy sauce pan bring remaining ingredients to a boil. Boil hard, stirring constantly for 3 minutes. Drain raisins and add to sauce. Boil another minute. Keep warm and serve over squares of gingerbread.

NOTES

MARINATED PORK TENDERLOIN

BUTTERED PEAS

SWEET POTATO PUDDING

BUTTERMILK MUFFINS

COCONUT PIE

PORK TENDERLOIN

whole <u>pork tenderloin</u> - 1 large or 2 small (about 3 pounds)

MARINADE:

¼ C soy sauce
¼ C <u>bourbon</u>
2 Tbsp brown sugar

Mix marinade ingredients and marinate pork several hours turning often. (See helpful hint # 22.) Remove meat from marinade and bake at 325 degrees for 1 hour - longer for large tenderloins. Carve in thin slices and serve with heated marinade. Serves 6.

Betty Rose Sexton

Note: This pork may also be served cold with a sauce of: ⅓ C sour cream, ⅓ C mayonnaise, 1 Tbsp dry mustard and 2 - 3 chopped green onions.

BUTTERED GREEN PEAS - Heat <u>2 cans of LeSueur peas</u> over medium heat. Drain. Add 3 Tbsp butter and salt to taste. Allow butter to melt and serve immediately.

SWEET POTATO PUDDING

4 C raw grated sweet potatoes
2 eggs - beaten
1 ¼ C milk
3 Tbsp flour
½ stick margarine - melted
1 tsp vanilla
1½ C sugar
¼ tsp salt

Melt margarine. Stir in flour until smooth. Add remaining ingredients leaving the grated potatoes until last. Mix well. Pour into a greased baking dish. Bake at 350 degrees for 1 hour. Serves 6.

BUTTERMILK MUFFINS

1 C buttermilk
¼ tsp soda
1 C self-rising flour
1 egg - beaten

Combine buttermilk and soda. Add flour, stirring until smooth. Beat in egg. Spoon batter into greased muffin tins. Bake at 425 degrees for 30 minutes. Makes 6.

COCONUT PIE

1 unbaked pie shell
2 C sugar
1 C butter less 2 Tbsp - softened
4 eggs - separated
2 C grated coconut
1 Tbsp cider vinegar
pinch of salt

Cream butter and sugar. Add egg yolks one at a time then coconut, vinegar and a pinch of salt. Beat egg whites until stiff and fold into mixture. Pour into an unbaked pie crust. Makes 1 large or 2 small pies. Bake at 350 degrees for 30 - 40 minutes or until center is set.

CAN-CAN CHICKEN
FRENCH-CUT GREEN BEANS
PINK ARTIC SALAD
FRESH APPLE MUFFINS
🍃 TOFFEE SQUARES

CAN-CAN CHICKEN

1 can cream of chicken soup
1 can cream of celery soup
1 soup can (1⅓ C) water
1 can (12 oz) or 1½ C diced cooked chicken
1⅓ C Minute Rice
1 can French fried onions

Combine all ingredients except onions in a large skillet. Bring quickly to a boil. Cover and simmer for 7 minutes. To serve, top with onions. Serves 4 - 6.

Margaret B. Almond

FRENCH-CUT GREEN BEANS

2 cans French-cut green beans
1 pkg slivered almonds
1 Tbsp instant beef bouillon

Drain green beans. Add enough water to cover. Stir in bouillon. Add almonds. Simmer about 10 minutes. Serves 6.

PINK ARTIC SALAD

8 oz cream cheese - softened
2 Tbsp mayonnaise
2 Tbsp sugar
1 can whole cranberry sauce
1 can (15 oz) crushed pineapple
1 carton (8 oz) Cool Whip

Add mayonnaise and sugar to cream cheese. Drain pineapple. Add fruit. Fold in Cool Whip. Put in individual molds or Pyrex dish. Freeze. Keeps well and does not get icy. (See helpful hint # 42.)

Mother, Elizabeth F. Easley

FRESH APPLE MUFFINS

2 C flour
½ C sugar
1 Tbsp baking powder
½ tsp salt
½ tsp cinnamon
½ tsp nutmeg
1½ C peeled, <u>chopped apples</u> - golden delicious

1 C milk
¼ C vegetable oil
1 egg - beaten
¼ C sugar
½ tsp cinnamon

Combine dry ingredients. Stir in 1 C of the apples. Make a well in center of mixture. Combine milk, oil and egg. Add to dry ingredients. Stir just until moistened. Spoon into greased muffin tins. Combine remaining ½ C apples, ¼ C sugar and ½ tsp cinnamon. Spoon over top of muffin batter. Bake at 350 degrees for 20 - 30 minutes. Makes 1 dozen.

Marie P. Jefferson
Danville, Virginia

TOFFEE SQUARES

2 C flour
1 C light brown sugar
1 stick butter (no substitutes) - softened
1 C <u>pecan pieces</u>

2 sticks butter (no substitutes)
¾ C light brown sugar
1 pkg (6 oz) <u>semi-sweet chocolate chips</u>

Combine flour, 1 C brown sugar and the softened butter with a pastry blender. Press into an ungreased 13 x 9 inch aluminum pan. Sprinkle with pecans. Combine 2 sticks butter and ¾ C brown sugar in a sauce pan. Bring to a boil and boil exactly 1 minute - stirring constantly. Pour immediately over crust. Bake at 350 degrees for exactly 20 minutes. Surface will be bubbly. Allow to cool for one minute. Sprinkle chocolate chips over the top. Allow chips to soften then spread with a knife to cover top. Chill then remove and bring to room temperature before cutting into squares.

The Words Worth Eating Recipe Collection
Ukrop's Super Market

AUTUMN

TARRAGON CHICKEN
BUTTER BEANS
CORN PUDDING
CRESCENT ROLLS
APPLE COBBLER

TARRAGON CHICKEN

2½ - 3 lb <u>whole chicken</u>
1 <u>clove garlic</u> - crushed
1 Tbsp tarragon
salt and pepper
1 stick margarine - melted
1 lemon - juiced
1 Tbsp tarragon

Rub chicken with salt and pepper. Place garlic and 1 Tbsp tarragon in cavity. Place the chicken on a rack in a greased pan with enough water to cover the bottom. Bake uncovered at 350 degrees for 1 - 1½ hours - until skin is golden and leg juices run clear when pricked. Combine melted margarine, lemon juice and tarragon. Baste several times while cooking. Remove chicken from oven and prick deeply with a fork. Pour remaining basting mixture over. Allow to stand a few minutes before carving. Serves 4 - 6.

Janet Coleman

BUTTER BEANS (baby limas)

2 pkgs or 1 poly bag of frozen <u>baby lima beans</u>

In a large sauce pan bring lightly salted water to a boil. Add butter beans and cook until tender - about 20 - 30 minutes. Partially drain, add 3 Tbsp margarine and season.

170

CORN PUDDING

2 cans whole kernel corn - drained
1 egg - beaten
½ C milk
½ C sugar
2 Tbsp flour
½ tsp salt
2 - 3 Tbsp margarine
nutmeg

In a large bowl sprinkle sugar and flour over corn. Gently stir. Add milk, beaten egg and salt. Pour into a greased baking dish. Dot with margarine and generously sprinkle with nutmeg. Bake at 350 degrees for 1 hour.

REFRIGERATOR CRESCENT ROLLS

Bake according to package directions.

APPLE COBBLER

1 can apple pie filling
1 C sugar
1 C flour
1 tsp salt
1 tsp baking powder
1 egg - beaten

Place apples in a greased square Pyrex baking dish. Sprinkle with cinnamon. Combine dry ingredients then stir in egg. Mix thoroughly - will be crumbly. Spread over apples. Bake at 350 degrees for 35 - 40 minutes. Serve warm with ice cream or a dollop of whipped topping. Serves 8.

SUPER CHICKEN CASSEROLE

4 - 5 chicken breasts - boned and skinned
olive oil
1 can cream of mushroom soup
1 C macaroni
¾ C milk
1 C sharp cheese - grated
1 pkg frozen chopped broccoli - thawed
salt and pepper to taste

Cut chicken into small pieces. Brown in olive oil. Remove and set aside. Cook macaroni in lightly salted water. (See helpful hint # 31.) Drain. Mix chicken pieces, soup, cooked macaroni, milk, broccoli and ½ C of the grated cheese. Season. Put into a greased casserole dish and top with remaining cheese. Bake at 350 degrees for 45 minutes. Serves 4 - 6.

Burrell Stultz

CHEESE SPOON BREAD

2 C milk
1 C cornmeal
¼ C margarine - soft
½ C sharp cheese - grated

4 eggs - separated - room
  temperature
1 tsp salt

Heat milk in heavy sauce pan over moderate heat. When milk is hot, slowly add cornmeal stirring constantly. Cook until thickened. This does not take long. Remove from heat. Stir in butter, cheese, egg yolks and salt. Beat egg whites until stiff and fold into cornmeal mixture. Pour into a greased 2 quart casserole. Bake at 350 degrees for 30 - 40 minutes. Serve immediately with plenty of butter.

ORANGE-PINEAPPLE SALAD

2 pkg (3 oz) <u>orange-pineapple gelatin</u>
1½ C boiling water
1 can (6 oz) <u>frozen orange juice</u>
1 can <u>mandarin oranges</u> - drained
1 small can <u>crushed pineapple</u> - with juice

Dissolve gelatin in boiling water. Add all other ingredients. Pour into a mold and refrigerate. Congeals quickly because of the frozen juice.

Eleanor F. Smart

OATMEAL SQUARES

⅓ C butter or margarine
⅔ C brown sugar
1 egg
1 C milk
1 C flour
¼ tsp baking soda
½ tsp salt
1¼ C <u>uncooked oatmeal</u>
1 pkg (6 oz) <u>chocolate chips</u>

Cream butter and sugar. Add egg - beat well. Add milk and dry ingredients. Reduce mixer speed and add oatmeal and chocolate chips. Spread in a greased 9" baking dish. Bake at 350 degrees for 25 - 30 minutes.

GLAZE:

½ C sugar
3 Tbsp lemon juice

Bring to a boil and pour over squares when removed from oven. Allow to cool before cutting.

1979 - Beverley H. Davis

A
U
T
U
M
N

SEAFOOD CASSEROLE

1 can cream of shrimp soup
¼ C mayonnaise
1 Tbsp grated onion
½ C milk
1½ lbs shrimp - cooked and cleaned
1 can (7½ oz) crabmeat - drained or ½ lb fresh
1 can sliced water chestnuts - drained
½ C chopped celery
1 C cooked rice
2 Tbsp minced fresh parsley
salt and white pepper
paprika

Combine soup, mayonnaise, onion and milk. Add remaining ingredients except paprika. Season to taste. Place into a greased shallow baking dish. Sprinkle generously with paprika. Bake at 350 degrees for about 30 minutes. Garnish with fresh parsley sprigs. This casserole may be stretched by adding more seafood and rice. Add milk, 1 Tbsp at a time, if it seems dry. Serves 6.

TOSSED SALAD

Use a variety of greens with halved cocktail tomatoes and chopped green onions. Add in a few sprigs of parsley and another fresh herb such as dill or basil if desired. Toss with an oil and vinegar dressing. (Good Seasons Italian - make as directed then add a generous dash of sugar.)

Jane Wootton

174

QUICK LITTLE LOAF

¼ C shortening
¼ C sugar
3 eggs - beaten
2 C flour
2½ tsp baking powder
1 tsp salt
1 C milk

Cream shortening and sugar. Add eggs one at a time mixing well after each. Combine dry ingredients and mix alternately with milk - adding flour first and last. Do not over mix. Bake in a greased and floured small loaf pan at 350 degrees for 45 - 50 minutes.

BETH'S APPLE PIE

½ C margarine - melted
1 ¼ C sugar
1 tsp cinnamon
dash allspice
dash nutmeg
¼ tsp salt
1 egg - well beaten
2 C peeled and chopped <u>apples</u> - <u>Golden Delicious</u>
1 <u>unbaked pastry shell</u>

Add sugar, spices and salt to melted butter. Mix well. Add beaten egg. Fold in apples. Pour into pastry shell. Bake at 400 degrees for 10 minutes. Reduce heat to 350 degrees and bake about 45 minutes longer. Serve with ice cream or a dollop of frozen whipped topping.

AUTUMN

BURGER 'N BEANS

2 strips bacon
1 small onion - chopped
1 lb ground beef
2 cans (16 oz each) pork and beans
½ C dark corn syrup
½ C catsup
½ C sugar
½ tsp dry mustard
1 Tbsp Worcestershire sauce
1 tsp salt

Cut bacon into small pieces. Cook bacon, onion and beef in heavy skillet. Drain. Mix with other ingredients. Pour into a greased casserole dish. Bake at 350 degrees for 30 minutes. Serves 6 - 8.

1978 - Tinsley O. Northen

APPLE SLAW

3 large apples - Golden Delicious - peeled and grated
1 lemon juiced
1 head cabbage - shredded
⅔ C mayonnaise
½ C sugar
½ tsp salt
¼ C golden raisins

Toss grated apple with lemon juice. Add cabbage and remaining ingredients. Mix well. Regrigerate. Serves 6 - 8.

CHEESE LOAF

2 C Bisquick
¾ C milk
¼ C sharp cheese - grated
3 Tbsp butter - softened

Blend Bisquick and milk. On a floured surface roll into a rectangle about ¼" thick. Spread with softened butter and sprinkle with grated cheese. Roll up jelly roll fashion. Place seam side down on a greased baking sheet. Cut about ⅓ of way through loaf every inch to make slices. Bake at 450 degrees for 20 minutes.

CARAMEL CHOCOLATE SQUARES

1 bag (14 oz) caramel candy
⅔ C evaporated milk - divided
1 German Chocolate Cake Mix
¾ C butter - softened
1 C chopped pecans
1 pkg (6 oz) chocolate chips

Combine caramels and ⅓ C evaporated milk in top of double boiler to melt. In the meantime, combine the cake mix, butter, remaining ⅓ C evaporated milk and pecans. Press half of this mixture into a greased sheet cake pan. Bake at 350 degrees for 6 - 10 minutes until firm. Sprinkle chocolate chips on top then pour on melted caramels. Crumble remaining cake mixture on top of this. Return to oven and bake 20 - 25 minutes. Cool slightly then chill in the refrigerator about 30 minutes before cutting into squares.

Sally Y. Garber (Mrs. Gerry)
Orlean, Virginia

A
U
T
U
M
N

STEAK and GRAVY

POTATO CASSEROLE

❧ TOMATO DELIGHT

POPPY SEED BISCUITS

❧ COCONUT MACAROONS

STEAK and GRAVY

1 round steak
flour for dredging
6 fresh mushrooms - sliced
1 can golden mushroom soup

Cut round steak into very thin strips. Dredge in heavily seasoned flour. Heat small amount of cooking oil in a large skillet or electric fry pan. Sauté mushrooms several minutes. Remove and reserve. Brown meat quickly on all sides. Remove and drain excess oil if necessary. Mix soup with 1 can water. Return mushrooms and beef to pan and pour soup over. Simmer for 1 hour or place in a Dutch oven in a 350 degree oven for 1 hour. Stir occasionally. Add more water if needed. Serves 4 - 6.

POTATO CASSEROLE

9 - 10 medium white pota-
  toes
1 tsp garlic salt
1 tsp onion salt
1 C sour cream
8 oz cream cheese - room
  temperature
½ stick margarine - melted
paprika

Boil potatoes until tender and mash until all lumps are gone. Add remaining ingredients and mix well. Place in a greased 1 quart casserole. Pour melted butter over top and sprinkle with paprika. Bake at 350 degrees until well heated - at least 30 minutes. May be made a day ahead. Serves 6.

Yvonne Dippel
Bettendorf, Iowa

TOMATO DELIGHT

"This is a nice substitute for fresh tomatoes in the off-season."

2 C <u>canned tomatoes</u>
1 pkg (4 oz) <u>strawberry gelatin</u>
1 Tbsp cider vinegar
2 tsp Worcestershire sauce
blue cheese dressing - optional

Cut tomato chunks into small bits. Heat tomatoes. Stir in gelatin until dissolved. Add vinegar and Worcestershire. Refrigerate until firm. Make individual servings on a bed of shredded lettuce with mayonnaise or blue cheese dressing. (See helpful hint # 42.) Garnish with peppers, onions, celery and/or cucumbers as desired.

Anne M. Grigg

POPPY SEED BISCUITS

1 can <u>refrigerator biscuits</u> - Dip each biscuit in melted butter then sprinkle with poppy seeds. Bake in a greased pan as package directs.

COCONUT MACAROONS

1 large bag <u>grated coconut</u>
1 can <u>sweetened condensed milk</u>
dash salt
<u>candied cherries</u>

Add just enough milk to coconut to hold it together. Add dash of salt. Drop by teaspoonfuls onto greased cookie sheet. Press a half of cherry into center of each. Bake at 350 degrees for about 10 minutes or until they begin to brown and are firm. Keeps well in a tightly covered tin.

AUTUMN

179

HAM STEAKS

2 - 3 <u>ham steaks</u>   1 C <u>pineapple juice</u>
1 Tbsp oil   1 Tbsp corn starch

Heat oil in an electric skillet or Dutch oven. Brown ham steaks 2 - 3 minutes per side. Drain. Pour off pan drippings. Mix the pineapple juice (from drained pineapple in recipe to follow) and cornstarch, stirring until dissolved. Pour over ham steaks and simmer about 20 minutes. Stir occasionally. Serves 4 - 6.

BRUSSEL SPROUTS

1 lb <u>fresh brussel sprouts</u> - Wash. Drop into lightly salted boiling water for about 8 - 10 minutes until just tender. Remove and drain. Gently toss with butter, and salt and pepper. Serves 4 - 6.

Mary Collins

PINEAPPLE BAKE

2 cans <u>pineapple chunks</u> -   1 roll crushed <u>Towne</u>
  drained   <u>House Crackers</u>
⅔ C sugar   1 stick melted butter or
5 Tbsp flour   margarine
2 C cheddar cheese -
  grated

Spread pineapple chunks in a greased shallow baking dish. Mix sugar and flour and sprinkle over pineapple. Spread cheese (See helpful hint # 4.) over this then cracker crumbs. Bake at 350 degrees for 30 minutes. Serves 8.

"Rich and delicious."
Margie Ayres

LIGHT MUFFINS

2 C Bisquick
¼ C sugar
2 Tbsp margarine - melted
1 egg - well beaten
¾ C milk

Combine dry ingredients. Make a well and stir in margarine, egg and milk with a fork. Stir only until moistened. Spoon into greased muffin tins. Bake at 400 degrees for 15 minutes or until golden brown. Freeze any left over for another meal or split and toast for breakfast. Makes 12.

NUTMEG POUND CAKE

1 box Duncan Hines Supreme yellow cake mix
1 pkg (3½ oz) instant vanilla pudding mix
⅓ C cooking oil
4 eggs
½ tsp nutmeg

Combine all ingredients in large bowl of electric mixer. (See helpful hint # 7 - add scant ½ tsp nutmeg if fresh is used.) Mix at medium speed for 2 minutes. Grease and flour tube Bundt pan. Bake cake at 350 degrees for 50 - 60 minutes. Cool in pan for 30 minutes then invert on serving platter. This cake is great as is or with a dollop of whipped topping dusted with nutmeg.

Elise Bridges

A
U
T
U
M
N

SCALLOPS AU GRATIN

BAKED ACORN SQUASH

GREEN BEAN CASSEROLE

POP-N-FRESH LOAF

&. BLACK FOREST CAKE

SCALLOPS AU GRATIN

1½ - 2 lbs <u>Bay scallops</u>
6 Tbsp margarine - divided
3 Tbsp flour
1 tsp instant chicken bouillon
1 tsp Dijon mustard
¼ tsp lemon juice
scant ⅛ tsp white pepper
1½ C milk
½ C pan juice from sauté
1 C grated <u>cheddar cheese</u> - divided
1 - 2 tsp chopped <u>fresh parsley</u>

Rinse scallops in salted water. Drain. Pat dry. Sauté in 3 Tbsp margarine until opaque. Remove with a slotted spoon to a greased 1½ quart flat baking dish. Reserve ½ C pan juices; discard rest. Melt remaining 3 Tbsp margarine. Add flour and allow to bubble about 2 minutes. Stir in bouillon, mustard, lemon juice, and pepper. Remove from heat. Stir in milk and pan juice until smooth. Return to heat and cook until thickened. Stir in ½ C grated cheese until cheese melts. Pour sauce over scallops. Top with remaining grated cheese. Bake at 400 degrees for 10 - 15 minutes. Sprinkle with parsley. Serve immediately. Do not over-cook. Serves 4 - 6.

The Words Worth Eating Recipe Collection
Ukrop's Super Market

BAKED ACORN SQUASH

2 acorn squash

Cut squash in half. Scoop out seeds. Cover a baking sheet with aluminum foil and grease heavily. Bake squash - cut side down - at 350 degrees for 45 minutes to 1 hour or until soft. Cut halves in two. Place a spoon of topping in center of wedge to serve. Serves 6 - 8.

TOPPING:
Mix together:

¼ C brown sugar   **½ stick melted margarine**
¼ C finely chopped pecans

GREEN BEAN CASSEROLE

2 cans (16 oz each) cut green beans	**⅛ tsp pepper**
¾ C milk	**1 can cream of mushroom soup**
½ tsp salt	**1 can fried onion rings**

Drain green beans. Mix milk, soup and seasonings then gently stir in beans. Bake in a greased casserole dish at 350 degrees for about 30 minutes. Top with onions and bake 5 minutes longer. Serves 6.

POP-N-FRESH LOAF

Refrigerator canned loaf of bread - Bake according to package directions. Serve on a wooden cutting board. Slice at the table.

BLACK FOREST CAKE

1 box Duncan Hines Devil's Food Cake Mix   **2 large cartons of Cool Whip**
1 can cherry pie filling

Make cake as package directs. Bake in 2 layers - 8 or 9 inches. When cooled, split layers. (See helpful hint # 23.) Spread between each layer ⅓ of the pie filling and cover with Cool Whip. Ice the entire cake with Cool Whip. Store in the refrigerator. May be made 1 - 2 days ahead.

AUTUMN

BAKED SPAGHETTI

1 lb box spaghetti
1 lb ground beef - cooked
1 large jar spaghetti sauce with mushrooms
1 tsp Italian Seasonings
mozzarella cheese slices
parmesan cheese

Cook spaghetti in a large pot of lightly salted water. Drain. Toss with several drops of olive oil. Combine spaghetti sauce and cooked ground beef. (See helpful hint # 2.) Add Italian Seasonings, salt and pepper. Mix with spaghetti. Place in a large greased baking dish. Cover with mozzarella slices. Bake at 350 degrees for 30 minutes. Leftovers may be frozen. (See helpful hint # 12.) Add parmesan cheese at the table. Serves 8.

TOSSED SALAD - Combine a mixture of lettuces: iceburg, bibb, endive. Add raw vegetables: carrots, radishes, tomatoes, mushrooms and onions. Add coarsely grated mozzarella cheese. Toss with a bottled Caesar dressing.

ITALIAN BREAD

Slice an Italian loaf of bread on the diagonal. Spread with soft butter. Wrap tightly in aluminum foil and heat in oven about 15 minutes.

PISTACHIO PIE

1 graham cracker crumb crust
1 pkg instant Pistachio pudding mix
1 can (15 oz) crushed pineapple
1 container (8 oz) Cool Whip

Make crumb crust by mixing 1 C crumbs with ½ C melted butter or margarine. Press into an 8 - 9 inch pie plate. Combine pudding mix and pineapple including juice until smooth. Fold in Cool Whip. Pour into crumb crust. Top with additional Cool Whip. refrigerate 2 - 3 hours or until firm.

Jo Elliott

NOTES

AUTUMN

NOTES

INDEX

ORDER ADDITIONAL COPIES

THE
"What in the World Are We Going To Have For Dinner?"
COOKBOOK
8 Berkshire Drive, Richmond, Virginia 23229

Please send ____ copies at $12.95 per copy _____

Shipping and handling $2.25 per copy _____

Va. residents add $0.58 sales tax per copy _____

Enclosed is a check for _____

(Make payable to Sarah E. Drummond)

Send to: Name _____

Street: _____

City: _____ State: _____ Zip: _____

A gift - Inscribe: To _____ From _____

ORDER ADDITIONAL COPIES

THE
"What in the World Are We Going To Have For Dinner?"
COOKBOOK
8 Berkshire Drive, Richmond, Virginia 23229

Please send ____ copies at $12.95 per copy _____

Shipping and handling $2.25 per copy _____

Va. residents add $0.58 sales tax per copy _____

Enclosed is a check for _____

(Make payable to Sarah E. Drummond)

Send to: Name _____

Street: _____

City: _____ State: _____ Zip: _____

A gift - Inscribe: To _____ From _____

Reorder Additional Copies

Save $1.00 on your reorder. Just send us the name, address, and phone number of the best stores in your town that sell cookbooks.

Name of Store _____

Owner or Manager's Name_____

Address _____

City _____ State _____ Zip_____

(Deduct $1.00 off your reorder when this is filled in)

Save $1.00 on your reorder. Just send us the name, address, and phone number of the best stores in your town that sell cookbooks.

Name of Store _____

Owner or Manager's Name_____

Address _____

City _____ State _____ Zip_____

(Deduct $1.00 off your reorder when this is filled in)